EMBRACING AMAZING

CONSCIOUSLY GROWING AN EMPOWERED FAMILY

DEBORAH AND JOHN LAHMAN

Paperback ISBN: 978-1-955090-12-4
eBook ISBN: 978-1-955090-15-5
Library of Congress Number: 2021917967

Published by the Unapologetic Voice House in Scottsdale, Arizona.

www.theunapologeticvoicehouse.com

CONTENTS

FOREWORD.. 1

INTRODUCTION... 3

CHAPTER 1 9
LEARNING TOGETHER

CHAPTER 2 33
HONORING

CHAPTER 3 64
BROKENNESS

CHAPTER 4 92
ENTREPRENEURIAL SPIRIT

CHAPTER 5 121
RESILIENCE

CHAPTER 6 150
THE VILLAGE

CONCLUSION 181
RESOURCES 185

ABOUT THE AUTHOR

After beginning their Indiana teaching careers, Deborah completed her Elementary Education Master's degree at Indiana University, while John earned his Master's in Secondary School Administration at Purdue University. When they moved to Arizona in 1988, they each pursued School Counselor Endorsements and shifted their public school endeavors from the classroom to Elementary and High School Counselor capacities.

Deborah and John retired after 25 years of public education careers and are now pursuing other ventures. Deborah launched her essential oils business Living Well Now and John moved his Lahman Financial Services business from part-time to full-time. As this book is released, their daughter Angela and son Aaron are primary partners with Deborah in Living Well Now while their son Andy is partnered with John in Lahman Financial Services.

In combining their wellness and wealth passions, business owner knowledge, and interpersonal counseling strategies, Deborah and John are enthusiastically mentoring others. They teach, empower, and equip communities to fulfill their goals of wellness, purpose, and abundance.

FOREWORD

As a veteran teacher for twenty years in public schools and in the Department of Defense Dependent Schools, I saw many parenting styles. As I entered the business world, I observed how many individuals were not tuned into their aspirations, confidence, sense of self and mindset. I'm fascinated with how many adults have blocked their own success and are not equipped with the skills and communication strategies to navigate the stressors of life. Now I have another twenty years as a business mentor and most of my time is spent on self-empowerment and teaching sales skills. I find it so interesting as these are also basic life skills for thriving.

So, when I met Deborah and John Lahman in the business arena, I caught myself drawn to their family. Their family modeled harmony, connection, love, sense of self, encouragement, integrity and other family dynamics that are all qualities we commonly strive toward as the family ideal. These are also entrepreneurial skills that draw people to you. I noticed how their grandchildren were integrated into their business lives in a healthy manner. Their dynamics of generational parenting were intriguing to me. These children were learning valuable skills and how to navigate life challenges in a healthy balanced way.

Through business events, I saw how people were also drawn to this family for support, mentoring and encouragement. In all actuality, they were gaining life skills and strategies not just for business. As former school counselors, John and Deborah demonstrate life strategies that help nurture people. These same skills were obvious within their family dynamics as well. I noticed how they used these with their grandchildren equipping them with interdependent skill sets, sense of self, respect for the family dynamic, communication skills, honesty and empathy.

The Lahmans' practice and share the habit of mindset intention. They model real life purpose that develops a generational legacy of healthy, emotionally equipped individuals who thrive in the world. This is why I know this book will build your family skills and strategies for effective communication to navigate life. These practiced experiences result in the development of a mindful family dynamic impacting generations to come.

Their family models it.

Connie Marie
Business Mentor, Speaker, Veteran Teacher,
Healing Home Educator

INTRODUCTION

"We are creating a resilient family while moving in kindness through brokenness."

To Our Dearest Reader,

Everyone has stories to share. We decided it was time to share ours. We first talked about writing a book on parenting about thirty-five years ago. Since that time, we've been organically collecting our expertise and now it's time to share it with you.

A dear friend has repeatedly reminded us of our goal and reinforced our notion of writing this book. She shares her belief about us in these words: "All people are to be celebrated and encouraged to be their best selves. John and Deborah understand this and intentionally act in ways that nourish self-images that are healthy and resilient." What an awesome invitation to take action to do what we have imagined after all these years.

We do have some insights and lessons to share that offer information about our journey to those who follow in the future.

And as we related in our dedication, we especially offer our words and insights for our grandchildren and their children and their children's children.

There's a reason we waited this long to put these words together. We just couldn't write this book while we were in the throes of parenting, building our family foundation, and nurturing our businesses. Besides, we were still collecting data—and we still are—even as grandparents.

We treasured what we learned from the experts, including something that really spoke to us:

Most of us think we have nothing original to say. Write anyway. We all have perspectives that are our own. By writing from our heart we share our lives with others. We build trust that our stories matter. If we learn to tell our stories we can learn how to live them.

It's what we heard inside ourselves as we read Henri J.M. Nouwen in *Bread for the Journey,* him inviting us to offer our perspectives unabashedly.

We have been intuitively and intentionally designing our lives around our dreams and goals since childhood. These personal visions have evolved and changed individually and collectively in concert with our family over more than forty-five years now. Our prayer is that by writing about the thoughts, learnings, understandings, revelations, musings, etc., that have informed our past . . . we are able to provide information and stimulation for discussion among numerous families for the present moment while providing some ideals, grounding, and values for future generations to come.

The relevance of this book is in our desire to both validate your journey and to offer hope and counsel for those of you who are parenting now or will follow in the years to come. Parenting is hard . . . the reality of parenting is that it is really hard. And let's be honest, if we're a parent, we do hard things. Creating a family is much more difficult than others seem to view it. We hope that you will take a few tangible strategies for your own journey.

We would like for this book to make a significant difference in your life, long term. In living our lives, whether we are purposeful about it or not, we leave a legacy behind. We create our legacy by the words we use, the choices we make, the paths we traverse. We humans are constantly intersecting and influencing one another in spontaneous, significant ways.

It is imperative that we first seek to understand ourselves, to look in the mirror and both acknowledge our strengths while also recognizing our limitations. When we own up to our natural attributes, seek to educate and enlarge our knowledge base, and gather the support of others, we can find success. As the parenting journey matures, if we're deliberate and persistent, we will have done most things well. Of course, that comes with the understanding that no one is perfect, life is messy, and things do go awry. Seeking to monitor and adjust our pathways becomes crucial as we navigate each challenging endeavor.

When kids are little, you dress them. As they get older, you might give them a choice between *this one* or *that one*. When Andy was a little guy, he would've preferred to wear a smooth cotton play shirt on Sunday. We found that if we stood him up on his dresser and helped him to button his *church* shirt we were able to manage the disruption. Some tears were shed and then he found out that shirts with buttons weren't that bad after all. In fact, he wears them regularly these days!

On the one hand, allowing the messy means we must trust in the process and focus more on allowing life to come to us. By contrast, when we live with purpose, we make decisions that help achieve specific outcomes. We trusted that there were some parenting moments over which we had little control and yet we appreciated such disruptions as serendipitous. By living intentionally while incorporating the unexpected into our lives, we created our legacy.

While we were creating that legacy, we never had all the answers or the best solutions. However, we did make the time to seek clarification and we strived for improvement. As our parenting minutes turned into hours, into days, months, and then years, we were in constant study of what was working and what wasn't. We were making adjustments on the fly.

We want to acknowledge how challenging and how difficult parenting can be if we go it alone. We believe in the value of giving folks opportunities to support one another. We become important to others when we offer encouragement in tough times.

In writing this book, we offer our perspectives and invite you to broaden yours. You have a lot to share. You can support others and they can support you. You're going to see we don't have it all figured out. At the same time, we've learned enough things that we want to share with the larger community. As you read, you'll find at the end of each chapter several tools that we have found effective.

This book will require work if you choose to engage it. That work will be worth the effort. There's work here because of the nature of life and the nature of living in a world full of change and transformation. As you encounter each chapter, you should read it knowing it is structured in a particular way. In each chapter, we've identified segments that reflect on child, parent, and community. Diving into each will help you see some stories from our journeys, as well as some targeted information about each area. You will find questions at the end of each chapter intended to help you engage the material, whether you're working solo through the book or in a book study with others.

Keep in mind that we're coming from a perspective as public educators/teachers/counselors and business creators. That's part of our fabric. Considering the energy we invested in education, we know firsthand the sense of responsibility that most teachers feel for the learning outcomes they desire for their students. And we feel the same about you. We expect you to seek outcomes you never dreamed possible.

We really love blending both the mind and heart of parenting and you will notice that in this book. We have placed a great deal of emphasis on teamwork. We recognize the importance of parents in the cohesive functioning of each family. As parents, we must ask: How are we the central hub for making things work smoothly? In order to produce a thriving child or family, we must commit to offering love, structure, discipline, and encouragement all rolled into our role as parent.

To expand our understanding, we have cultivated relation-ships with many folks from various walks of life. Family, friends, and neighbors have been important to us. We've learned a lot from them. We've also sought outside experts with whom to consult. They've helped us grow in our personal and profes-sional lives and in our parenting journeys. Some of what we've taken away from these sessions have strengthened our own re-lationship and in turn strengthened our family.

As we have instilled consistency in our family, we have fo-cused on driving our stake in matters of importance, taken on new challenges as opportunities arose, and stayed willing to make paradigm shifts in seeking to fulfill many of our dreams. We have passionately added wellness strategies, personal de-velopment experiences, financial stewardship initiatives, and parenting tools to our toolbox over the years. Each of these has stretched us to the outcomes we share with you in the pag-es ahead.

So please enjoy, learn and grow while you read. We hope you fall in love with our family. Angela, Andy and Aaron have grown up to be incredible adults and entrepreneurs themselves.

As you engage with our book, may you be inspired to build a thriving, beautiful, imperfect family unit.

From our thriving family to yours,
John and Deborah Lahman

CHAPTER 1

LEARNING TOGETHER

*"We are interconnected by communicating
intentionally and clearly in an affirming way."*

Very well-meaning older friends of ours persistently told us, "Just wait until you see what's next. . . the worst parenting challenges are up around the corner." As we concluded the diaper days, we were informed that preschool and primary years were impossible. As kindergarten ended, the pitfalls of parenting primary ages were being underscored. Of course, we knew that a five-year-old doesn't function on the same level as a ten-year-old! And later, as we stood at the advent of having one or more teenagers in our family, all of the horrors of parenting high-schoolers were unloaded on us.

Not that we didn't appreciate all of the well-meaning utterances, but it was a bit unnerving and overwhelming at times. Just when we thought we were thankfully and successfully closing one chapter, folks were pointing out to us the even greater challenges that were ahead.

We chose to turn those challenges into opportunities. We trusted God that we would have the necessary skills for what we would face in the years ahead. And of course, that means choices.

COMMUNITY SUPPORTED

Every day, we have choices. Every choice sets an intention toward an outcome. Every step we take leads us in the direction of that outcome. We can put one foot in front of the other randomly or we can do so with purpose . . . with intention. If we know where we want to go, then our stepping forward requires foresight. One step can seem little for some while one step can seem massive for others. This is why, at times, we need to take steps smaller than regular steps; baby steps! We inch our way forward in the direction that we wish to go.

Choosing our steps helps us to be proactive. We can create greater congruity in our lives by action planning toward our goals and then taking those actions that bring the goals to fruition. When we choose goals in alignment with desired outcomes, we give ourselves the opportunity to create a more fully thoughtful, holistic life.

While almost all parents will make some changes from the way in which they were parented . . . most of us end up parenting as we were parented. Similarly, as parents, our school experiences have a significant impact on how we anticipate our children will experience school. And the fact is that there can be a world of difference between a parent's memory of their school days and the school life their children will experience. A parent's good or bad memories could give way to alternate outcomes for their kids. The opportunity to improve on one's parenting is by taking a step back from the role and considering objectively his or her parenting strategies. We learned these things through professional development or by finding people we saw doing this well and asked them to walk alongside us, literally and figuratively. There are many fond memories of taking evening walks with our dear friends, chatting about things we were experiencing as parents.

As we proceed along the parenting journey, we know good communication is critical. And it involves both talking and listening. Listening to the voices of children in our homes means growing with children as they mature. Listening as a parent is like a roller coaster ride. There are surprises galore with kids. Children are growing physically, emotionally, and spiritually every day. As this growth is occurring, parents are challenged to adapt with the children. In the same way that we need to adapt, whether on the job or self-employed, when our business changes and evolves, so must we flex with our children as well. Parents must ride the roller coaster with their children, through the peaks and valleys that are created by this developmental process. Parents must choose how they will support their child(ren) to dream big and develop goals to reach their full potential.

We are acutely aware that current U.S. culture has an excess of stimuli. Screen time has replaced family communication on many levels. Shared meals are not as common. Casual parent-child interaction has lessened. Family mutuality has been reduced as all of us seem to understand *me* much more than we comprehend *we*.

We are distracted. Everything is fighting for more of our attention. When business owners get distracted, they see the issue in the numbers, clients and productivity. When it happens in our families, the effects can show up less obviously, and by the time we realize we have not made them a priority, oftentimes, it can be too late.

While social media now allows us to feel connected to/aware of what our friends are doing, there is far less engaging and lots more watching. This makes parenting an increasingly complex responsibility. We are growing while our children grow. We make our best decisions in the moment. Yes, we stumble, and they stumble. We can get discouraged. In our parenting years, we trusted that our hope and resilience would allow us to meet the challenges that came our way. That faith is no different now for this generation than it was for our generation.

We must all work together for our children's good if they are going to be successful.

THREE-LEGGED STOOL

Just as the dairy farmer—before the age of milking machines—depended on his three-legged stool to support him for the work at hand, schools similarly depend on parents to support their students and teachers. In our role as educators, we witnessed that the three-legged stool was not always being held up equally by all three legs and realized that a partnership among student, teacher, and parent was imperative for school success.

This three-legged stool concept says so much about building the bridge of relationship between teacher or the community, parent, and child, which is why we have organized our chapter to reflect each of these elements. As educators ourselves for fifty years combined, we saw numerous variations in these relationships. We saw some children who didn't have support at home and yet had support at school. Two legs on a stool makes it wobbly, shaky, and unstable. The same situation could be a family that felt that the school didn't support them or their child's needs.

In education, achievement and effective learning can best be accomplished when all parties are involved in the solution. When there is a strong cohesion between a community- supported, teacher-directed and child-centered approach, the stool will stand up easily and be strong enough to survive and thrive in any tough situation in which our children might find themselves.

PARENT DIRECTED

DRIVING OUR STAKE

There is a phrase that has been significant to us through the years: driving our stake. Driving a stake in construction language delineates a property line, or could be a site for a home's foundation. A stake signifies a fixed location or a permanent point of intention. In our terms, it focuses around where we center our interest and personal concern for something or someone. We drove our stake in both providing for our children and in seeking the best for them long-term both at home, and as you will see later in the book, in our various business ventures.

Most decisions were influenced by where we drove our stake in pursuing positive outcomes for our family. We were tenacious in our planning and organizing to see that our children would get our very best. And our family calendar reflected that. It documented and clarified our priorities in tracking activities from school concerts to sporting events to our own professional obligations. The family calendar represented our commitment to one another and symbolized the ways in which we were a team in accomplishing everyone's goals.

We prioritized being the kids' teachers in their preschool years. We felt it most important to be home to care for them during those formative years. And we felt doubly blessed to have an amazingly nurturing preschool offered by our local congregation. Once the formal school years began, our intentions began to flow into these new educational opportunities.

We wanted the best for Angela, Andy, and Aaron and we gave a great deal of attention and intention to these matters on a regular basis. When we first graduated from college, we were classroom teachers. Having been educators ourselves, we held some insights that helped us to both support educators and to work within the public school system to encourage great learning experiences, not just for our kids but all kids.

While some parents with less interaction with school norms might be intimidated by the school environment, we were genuinely interested in being involved. When you feel intimidated, you tend to hold back. You might stay away from that which you fear or don't fully understand. We believe that getting positively involved is important. Such action shows your child that you care about them and you support their successful educational opportunities. As we've discussed, the three-legged stool just doesn't function properly if parents turn their backs on their kid's school life.

In recent years, the term *helicopter parents* has gained traction. It refers to those who just can't stay away and feel the need to look out for any little thing that doesn't go their child's way. They helicopter more in a reactive way than proactive. We sought to be the latter, not the former. We chose to help honor the child in encouraging them for educational success by working cooperatively with each child's teacher.

Helicopter parents are typically over-engaged and seem to want to make school a one-legged stool. Rather than empowering their child, parents enable them when they hover. They are at the opposite extreme from those who turn their back and ignore their partnership with the school, thus leaving their child to fend for themselves. Neither a one-legged stool nor a two-legged stool can stand. Balancing the stool happens when parent, child, and teacher work cooperatively to promote academic and social successes.

VERSATILITY

As parents, sometimes it feels like we're just navigating chaos as our goals mean being in more than one place at a time. Instead of telling our children they could only be involved in one thing, we encouraged them to be as versatile as possible. That was a stake of ours with the intention of allowing them to grow and diversify their activities and associations.

In one situation, Angela had a choir performance the same night as a basketball game. So with the help of the coach and the choir director, she played in the majority of the basketball game, took a shower, and got dressed in the car on the way to sing her gorgeous heart out that evening.

There is further evidence of how we worked together creatively. In the early '90s, Andy and Aaron served as ball boys for the varsity football team at John's school. On Friday nights, they had to come straight from club swim team practice directly to kickoff. John was already on campus with his soccer team, guiding parking duties. Deborah would pick up the boys, with food for them, ensuring they had sufficient nourishment for their evening duties.

Our family calendar was vital to the success of our stake being driven so firmly. That didn't mean that it didn't feel chaotic, and that didn't mean that there weren't times we felt pulled in a variety of directions. When we saw how tight our schedules were going to be, we tried our best to be prepared for what was happening that day. Planning ahead seemed to be the best way to attack our busy schedules during those days. The challenge is to spend enough time together with the family calendar to sort out priorities and make good choices. Is it a little crazy at times? Yes. However, by working together and assessing needs, with flexibility, creativity, and good coordination, much can be achieved.

We sought to take the best of what our own parents offered us in our growing up years and then added our own flavor to the recipe. When we consider that every human being is constantly changing, that is magnified in the development of children and complicates the parenting journey. An infant and a toddler have different sets of needs. A third grader and a seventh grader are miles apart. And a teenager—in high school—is living with one foot in expanding social circles outside the family. All of these developmental milestones make parenting complicated. That's why we sought out resources to educate ourselves—and help others—to manage the journey creatively.

Communication is the front-seat driver in most family matters. How we outwardly express ourselves . . . or what it is that we don't say . . . has ripple effects. Our communication creates outcomes. We all know that it takes a driver's license to get behind the wheel of a car to go anywhere unaccompanied. The licensed driver has received instruction and some hands-on experiences to better prepare for going down the road.

In the same way, where family health and wellness are concerned, just imagine if parents either chose or were required to get a parenting license when they brought a child into their family. Such a license would assure that they would be introduced to information that could better help them to steer their family down the roadway. Like driving, the parenting road is curvy, there are potholes, and occasionally the road will be closed. However, getting through, while bringing the best outcomes to kids and families, is the ultimate intention.

As parents, we know that parenting was our toughest job ever —and also the most important. As school counselors, we met and worked with parents who were seeking help on their parenting journey. Sometimes, we found parents upset with teachers or teachers confused by parents' choices and behaviors. And we sought to do something about it. We knew the important role that parents played in children's school success. We chose a creative, intentional *design* path rather than staying stifled in *default* mode, and we found partners readily available to see our kids through.

Use these questions to track information and get to know each of your kids' new teachers:

1. What is the best way to make contact with you? (Email, phone, virtual meets?)
2. Why did you get into teaching?
3. What are your expectations of your students and their families?
4. How can we help you as equal owners of our child's education?
5. Is there anything that you or your classroom needs that we can help you get or ways we could volunteer in order to encourage successes this year?

CHILD CENTERED

BUILDING FOR SCHOOL SUCCESS

From the beginning, we were intent to partner with the schools to create a positive learning environment for each of our children. In our earliest parenting years, while surviving on one income, we had a sum total of nine years of K-12 teaching experience under our belts. We understood the importance of being not just interested but also proactive in partnering with the school to help ensure successful learning opportunities for our children.

When Angela went off to kindergarten, we spoke up as parents when we realized her teacher was under a great deal of pressure due to an over-enrolled classroom. We worked with the teacher and brought our concern to the principal as well. Eventually, an aide, an extra adult in the classroom, was added to help assist every learner and provide greater one-on-one attention for these young children just beginning their school years. We sought and achieved a win-win outcome, helping the teacher get some assistance while ensuring an even healthier learning environment for not just Angela but also every student in that classroom.

And later as it turned out, our positive activism manifested into an invitation from the school's superintendent to serve on a Gifted Students' Task Force in order to help implement educational enrichment for our children and others in the school. This turned out to be a great way for us to stay invested as people who valued education. By focusing on partnering with the school staff, we were able to better ensure good learning environments for our own children within the school system.

For most parents, when their children first go to school, there is a mix of emotions. We may feel sad, happy and confused—all at the same time. We understand the difficulty of when and how kids should start school because, while it felt complex, with regard to Andy and Aaron, we felt certain about when to have them start school, because of our own educational journeys.

We gave priority to building a strong foundation by honoring each child's sense of self. For example, we ultimately chose for both Andy and Aaron to start school almost a year later than some of their peers. They had May and August birthdays, respectively. We made this decision in order to give them the very best foundation for success that we thought possible. As their parents, we had our own experiences to draw upon in making these decisions.

When we became school-age per our respective state guidelines, we both started school early. This meant feeling like we were often a step behind our peers, whether athletically or academically. Both of us finished high school at age 17 and didn't turn 18 until the first semester of college.

Deborah, with an August birthday, remembered being in the advanced math class when in high school, while not feeling like she had quite enough time to master concepts and skills. As she looks back, it would have been beneficial to be in the grade-level appropriate class in order to have support to hone the skills that came more quickly to her peers.

November baby John went to first grade (no kindergarten in those days) at age five and started his senior year of high school at age sixteen. In college, he went to Barcelona, Spain, for his Junior Year Abroad at the age of nineteen. He found himself overwhelmed with fellow students, many of whom were already twenty-one. He was chronologically, academically, and socially behind his peers.

As the youngest in our classes through the years, and with the various challenges we faced in both learning and maturity, we opted for Andy and Aaron to delay public school and complete one extra year of preschool. With spring and summer birthdays, respectively, it turned out that both of them were age six when they started kindergarten. Our extended family questioned why we were 'holding our boys back.' Actually, we focused on honoring the child in front of us . . . not tradition, not what everyone else was doing . . . with the hope of giving Andy and Aaron a little more time for maturation and confidence that would serve them for many years to come.

Another basis for our decision, besides our own personal experiences, was from Deborah's take on teacher perspectives she had encountered. As an elementary teacher in Indiana, she found colleagues talking about *summer birthday boys* struggling with concepts and learning. When she taught in Illinois, teachers started talking about *fall babies* and she quickly learned that December 1 was the enrollment cutoff. That only cemented our decision to better honor Andy and Aaron for future successes. We strongly believe we best honored Andy and Aaron by delaying their start in public school and assuring a strong foundation for their future.

Sometimes, in parenting and in life, you may have to break from tradition and go with the information that you have in front of you. This applies whether it concerns what is best for your child(ren) or whether it's about what's trending business-wise in your company domain.

1. While we have already emphasized the importance of parents becoming familiar with the teacher's behavioral expectations, academic curriculum, homework patterns, etc., it is also important for teachers to consider ways to provide support for the parents and families of their students.

2. If you are a teacher/educator, use these questions to track information about families of your students:

3. What do you and your family do in your free time?

4. Is there anything that I should know about your family which would help me understand your child better?

5. How can I best partner with your student to encourage their educational successes?

6. Are there any services you or your family needs currently that I can direct your way? (college, career counseling, language services, special education needs, etc.)

7. Who is the best person to contact when there is something we want to communicate with you? What is the best way to contact you?

We also suggest going to the teacher website to become familiar with it. If the school sponsors a Meet the Teacher night, be there. When Parent-Teacher conferences are scheduled, make time to attend. We promote getting on campus and becoming familiar with the surroundings and places that your children experience on a daily basis. The more a parent becomes accustomed to the school, the teacher(s), and the administration, the more likely the student will feel supported to be successful!

We did our best to stay in touch with teachers through the years, both to thank them for working with our kids and to ask questions when academic or personal issues surfaced. Honoring the school system and staff is paramount to undergird our children's success and to keep the stool upright!

EXTRACURRICULAR

Another means to cementing the family adaptability for school success is via extra curricular involvement. In some cases, that would involve a club, a sport, a musical group, theater opportunities, etc. Helping your child to be engaged outside the regular school day enhances their opportunities for healthy activity and positive social interactions.

As we lived our life by design, we did so by including our kids in decision-making. We encouraged extracurricular endeavors including music and sports. We discussed the choices they had and let them know we would be their biggest cheerleaders. This led to supporting them in many ways as we became soccer dad and soccer mom. We also became violin students, alongside our kids, and spent numerous weekend mornings trying to stay warm at winter swim meets. All a result of giving our kids a voice in their activities.

When our kids were little (preschool and primary grades), we were blessed to have a violin program available in our community. Our kids started with box violins and moved up to real instruments in due time. At a very tender age, appreciating music while becoming comfortable in performance and on stage was an extra blessing. We knew that getting on stage in front of others would prepare them for the confidence needed, regardless of whether they chose to follow our footsteps into education or into entrepreneurship or most any other endeavor.

Making decisions about which activities to choose or support for children is challenging for parents. A high school classmate said to us a few years ago, "Our parenting philosophy was to keep our kids so busy with academics and extracurricular activities that they really never had a chance to get in trouble!"

While we weren't scheming, we did seek ways for our kids to be involved, that's for sure. It wasn't just for the sake of being busy. We paid attention to the things towards which the kids gravitated. However, trying new things was always on the menu because we knew that developing a passion means needing to taste a bit of everything before ordering what you like. We chose for them to learn and explore a wide breadth of opportunities in order to see and experience a wide variety of performance-based and individual endeavors to expand their skill sets.

We chose for them to pursue extra-curricular options to broaden their life experiences. Activity by activity, our kids were getting learning opportunities and wider dimensions of self-awareness. We were seeking to help build kids who were well rounded and balanced. To supplement their academic pursuits, we expected them to supplement their school day with other interests. We also sought for them to gain relationship experiences including building friendship bonds with others who were pursuing similar activities. From extracurricular experiences, they were seeing the bigger picture and keeping a big vision for all that life could offer them in their school days and for the rest of their lives.

These were among some of the primary extracurricular experiences they chose:

1. Violin lessons
2. Piano lessons
3. Club swimming
4. Little League baseball
5. Choir
6. Theater/Thespians
7. Cross Country/Track
8. Softball
9. Faith-based camps/retreats/conferences
10. Tennis
11. Student Council
12. Basketball
13. Soccer
14. Football
15. Band
16. Show Choir
17. Chamber Singers
18. Volleyball

Our grandson, Grant, loves his extracurricular activities and has exhibited a focused learning approach that wows us. Initially in his relationship with building blocks. Whether putting an advanced block kit together or just free building, he proved adept at quick assembly while exhibiting maximum patience and an ability to see the end result through to completion. He needed little to no help ever.

While lots of kids (and adults) have enjoyed toys in many of the same ways, Grant has applied his mastery strategies to other areas as well. In coin collecting, he has combed thousands of coins and instantly can tell you whether one is just average or whether it is precious in age, limited production, or value.

Over the last couple of years, he has made himself a master fisherman – and mostly self-taught because the family members who have supported him weren't into fishing before. Not only does he catch fish, he can tell you all there is to know about kinds of fish, types of fishing gear, bait, lures, etc.

While we couldn't possibly predict where his ability to focus and learn will take him, we expect he will know everything there is to know about his next skill or trade. We will learn it with him.

TOOLS

As is commonly expressed, when you teach, you learn a great deal. Because we were parent educators, we found ourselves not just teaching but also learning and growing right along with our students. These teaching sessions served as opportunities to practice the skills and share our expertise while we were still in the trenches, facing our own parenting challenges.

Besides listening, offering verbal support is crucial to helping our children feel supported. We frequently let our kids know our appreciation for their choices. They knew they had our support amid the challenges. Schooling is a mixture of emotions for young people and it is a time when parents need to hang on and step up. If we are going to teach them to take the good with the bad, then we need to have a plan on how to maximize the good and minimize the bad. As you've read in this chapter, we care a great deal about intentional parenting. Here are a few of the strategies we were intentional about.

Study and Read: Many come to their parenting responsibility with little or no information or insight for the job ahead. We grant that some individuals come to parenting with limited preparation, but those who choose this journey must be centered and thoughtfully grounded to undertake such challenges.

We encourage parents to actively seek to better understand themselves. Many are those parents who say to themselves that they will change, modify, or eliminate some of the parenting that was done to them. They don't consider their parents as failures, but they certainly know at least one or more parenting strategies that they won't be handling in the same way their parents handled it when they were growing up. Many of us, however, have caught ourselves – more than once – in our own parenting, saying or doing exactly what we said we would never do to our children. What's that about? It's all about the fact that we do unto others what was done unto us.

Positive Affirmations: We found that affirmations provided the greatest return on our parenting investment. One of these was: *Work Hard and Have Fun.* No matter the activity, *work hard and have fun* was encouragement to do your best and enjoy the process. Secondly: *If I were you, I'd be proud of myself.* Regardless of the outcome of a homework assignment, or a test, or a *Turkey Trot* performance, we continued to emphasize the importance of giving your best and being pleased with the results. Being proud of personal effort keeps performance acceptance inside of oneself, not dependent on external influences. If they only acted to make us proud of them, then they would not be in touch with their own self-actualization.

Here are some affirmations:

1. Work hard and have fun.
2. If I were you, I'd be proud of myself.
3. I choose how I feel about my day.
4. I can learn from people in my community if I am willing to reach out.
5. Every day is a new beginning.

Set Goals: When it comes to parenting, setting positive goals in the midst of some of the challenges keeps strong relationships between parent(s) and children. As we expressed earlier, if we focus our energies in the beginning of our kids' learning journeys, they are more likely to flourish. As a parent, emphasizing proactive, anticipatory steps can head off future complexities and issues that stunt those expanding/developing minds.

CLOSING

It is important that we do all we can to make the best of all the years we have with our children!

Good, strong families are not born, they're developed as parents take into account their own school and personal stories while nurturing their children positively. There is no perfect recipe that will build the optimum family. We admit that while we were able to instill a lot of great things within our own family, there were plenty of shortcomings along the way. The more we tried, the more we figured out our mistakes and were able to compensate and adjust.

No parenting blueprint fits all. We know that "our" way may not be your way. However, taking the process one day at a time while keeping long-term goals front and center can bring about bridge-building outcomes that can serve children for a lifetime. We don't always have to know the final destination for us to take a step forward with intention.

We may be unsure of our kids' futures. However, we can stop, figure out a plan for our child's learning tomorrow and take a step towards that. So get out and take those steps, one foot in front of another, towards what is best for your children today. If we keep taking step after step, then one day, we can look back on the journey that we began and realize that we have come a long way, even if we thought we could have never made it so far.

So walk on...and know that we are walking with you!

REFLECTION QUESTIONS

How am I making the best choice. . .

1. To determine in what setting my child learns best?

_____

_____

_____

_____

2. To be supportive of my student's teacher(s)?

_____

_____

_____

_____

3. In the participation of programs and events at my child's school?

_____

_____

_____

_____

4. In the learning that comes home after the school day?

_____

_____

_____

_____

5. In enhancing my students' social learning in extracurricular activities?

_____

_____

_____

_____

CHAPTER 2

HONORING

*"We believe we are interdependent and honoring
of each member of our family through intentional
attitudes and behaviors in order to thrive."*

One of our first intentions as parents was to honor the three precious, unique gifts to us we named Angela, Andrew, and Aaron. Even though they are all grown up now and we are grandparents, when they were little, we knew that we wanted the best for them as they represented God's love given into our care. When we looked at their tiny toes, their tiny fingernails and their smiles, we had evidence that the creator had placed divine life, love, spirit, and purpose into each of them.

While in college, our youngest son, Aaron, studied yoga and traveled throughout India. He taught us that the Hindu expression *namaste* means "I bow to the Divine in you." Namaste says more about honoring, to us, than any other word or phrase in any language. Recognizing the inimitable creation represented by every human being stands as our premise about life on this planet. In discussing the divine in all of us, we must equally talk about how to honor that divine whether at home or at work. Beyond our family, we spent multiple decades honoring the marvelous potential in our students in our roles as school counselors, teachers and youth leaders.

Understanding the Divinity of each life is foremost in our understanding. Recognizing the beautiful creation that each human offers to others and to the world in total is super important. If we begin our parenting by seeking to acknowledge and recognize each unique soul entrusted to us, then we offer our very best energy and enthusiasm for the journey. Namaste encourages us to recognize the Divinity in one another on a very deep level. When we come into parenting with that perspective, we are better able to shower love, support, and encouragement on our kids. And not just daily, but for a lifetime! Honoring others, particularly our children, speaks volumes about mutual respect and love for one another.

HONOR AND RESPECT

I know that we have all heard the religious text, "Honor thy father and mother." So what does it look like to honor our children?

We honor them by:

1. Seeing the good in them.
2. Listening when they speak.

3. Creating an environment where they can feel safe and cared for physically, socially and emotionally.

A lot of parents believe that we honor our kids because they are a reflection of us; however, that isn't the impetus. That is simply the side effect. We honor the children in front of us because of the light we believe they have inside. It's the knowledge that they will grow up and use that light to do incredible things with their lives. We know this because we had that same light inside of us that people in our lives honored and thus helped us shine brightly.

Mutual Respect is a concept that is not just applicable to adults. Parents and children can find ways to respect each other. Respect is closely related to empathy, which really means that we can put ourselves in the shoes of the other. We have been where our kids have been, so listening with empathy expresses mutuality which in turn honors that light inside of them.

COMMUNITY SUPPORTED

NO LABELS

In our family's health journey, we wanted to only eat from a healthy place, so we've gotten really good at reading labels because we know that any packaged food can have many ingredients. Reading the labels on a food product can be extremely important . . . so that we know what we're consuming. If the food package looks yummy but it's full of salt, sugars, starches, etc., then we might decide there are other, better choices to make. When it comes to children, the same labeling process may or may not be at all helpful for the child or for the family itself.

We understand labeling has its purposes. Without question, this was an early learning experience for us on our parenting journey. In fact, we continue to share it to this day as we have opportunity because it has the potential to positively or negatively impact a child's wellbeing during their formative years.

Whenever a parent or teacher refers to a child as bold or shy or brilliant or incorrigible or lazy or gifted, that child may begin to wear that label as a personal trait similar to a food product label, only with much greater consequences. It may seem harmless, but the potential to either help or hurt the child is enormous. In most cases, a positive label is better because a child can resonate with any suggestion that he or she is capable, charming, loving, helpful, competent, or any number of other positive traits. In our generation, we sometimes referred to complimentary messages as "warm fuzzies" because they are supportive and encouraging. Disrespectful or negative comments were known as "cold pricklies" because the recipient is left feeling inadequate or less than capable. We whole-heartedly acknowledge that a "warm fuzzy" almost always feels better than any "cold prickly." More praise than persecution is always the right formula!

In a slightly different vein, a parent who says about her child "well, she has trouble reading because I did," or "he's no good in math and neither was I" sends a clear message to the child that he or she is going to find a particular skill difficult to learn, let alone master. This may provide the child with an excuse — an out —and may prevent him or her from ever tackling the subject or skill with much energy or hope. This is failure by association rather than allowing a child to experience the subject for her/himself and learn it for themselves. If you perceive that you will not be successful, why even try? This is clearly a point where parents need to evaluate their own childhood experiences and not label their kids as *just like me* without full effort and determination.

Our suggestion in this arena is to keep from putting any kind of limiting label on a child or young person. On the one hand, we understand that there may be value in being positive and complimentary. At the same time, putting any limits on a child by labeling can be potentially damaging. Any name or adjective expressed by any individual, whether parent, teacher, peer, or extended family member, that puts the child in a restrictive box has the potential to limit that child's academic success or positive personal accomplishments. If a child feels stung by any negative term, then the child could end up owning the label for a lifetime. While most labels are used negatively a label can be informative which is used to support the child, not harm them.

We also knew of a student with both physical and academic challenges. The school nurse told us that this student had the most limited respiratory challenges of any student on campus. Yet this student came to school regularly, served very capably as a sports team manager, graduated high school, furthered their education, and is a valued staff

Labels of any kind carry connotations. They serve to isolate an individual or deride one's character. If we describe someone as *all talk, no action,* you take away a perception of this person as lazy whether or not you ever knew them personally. Being extremely cautious around labels of any kind is prudent. *No labels* was our motto so that our kids did *not* feel pigeon-holed with only certain strengths or demeaned due to academic, physical, or behavioral tendencies.

CARE

These days, peer bullying among school-age kids is an incredibly huge topic. Peer bullying frequently centers on labels. A bully will find another child's sensitivity point and then target this vulnerability in an unrelenting fashion. Great effort is being made in most school settings to recognize such behavior and put a stop to it. It's helpful to recognize that school bullies have usually been bullied themselves. They are repeating behaviors they have experienced. In some situations, we chose to confront the bully.

Social media has greatly enlarged the bully /victim scenario. While bullying used to just be in person, that has now become a reality on various social media platforms. Some of that bullying is overt and obvious. Much of it can just be implied and frankly, sometimes misunderstood by its context. As parents, paying attention to situations and being tuned in to our teens today is critically important to head off damaging digital relationships.

Of course, some children choose to be victims and must learn how to stand up for themselves. As school counselors, we sought to empower young people to advocate for themselves in positive ways. We also intervened to provide mediation between students to seek to change behaviors positively.

ENCOURAGEMENT BEYOND PRAISE

In a related arena close to self-pride, we find that being encouraging to our children is more honoring. If all we do is pour profuse praise on their heads, they may or may not own it for themselves. Encouragement of the child is better than praise of the action, for example: as opposed to saying, "that was a great pass," it may be better to say, "you passed the ball well." Giving ownership to the child and his or her execution of the action says more about their actual performance.

Andy was an excellent baseball player. And he was playing on a very talented team in his second Little League season. Expectations were high. And he found his way into the starting lineup as a second baseman and occasionally, as a pitcher. He was steady and handled the ball well when it came his way. We were his best encouragers without making a big deal about how important he was to this championship team. If we had been praising to excess or hyping his status, it might have gone in one ear and out the other. Or it may have focused his performance on our approval and less on his own satisfaction with a job well done.

All of our kids were multi-sport athletes. Not only were they competitive, but they had a high degree for excellence. Angela, as the oldest, kept the expectations for herself high. That's a great thing but along with that comes finding it hard to accept praise. So when basketball games didn't go as planned or when track and field times weren't as good as she hoped they would be, that's when encouragement became the most vital.

When it comes to praise and encouragement, it's important to pay attention to how we are appreciative and complimentary. Many parents seem to find it much easier to find things to criticize rather than the other way around. Keep encouraging for the sake and emotional health of each child.

We have made a habit of being complimentary of one another. As we've expressed previously, it's certainly easier to be critical and find fault with one another than it is to be positive. However, we know loving one another is still the greatest commandment. One of the best means for creating positivity has been appreciation. And most commonly, we have been quite faithful at sharing that on one's birthday. So when it's your birthday we're celebrating, besides a card or a gift, your consistent treat was hearing those of us around you share our appreciation of you.

On his sixth birthday, those of us who were present will always remember our grandson Dasan really experiencing appreciation fully. He had chosen his dining preference of Peter Piper Pizza for his family birthday party. Between games and pizza, we all surrounded him at the table and each of us took turns telling him how much we appreciated his abundant energy, his gentle hugs, his soccer talents, his loving eyes, etc. Dasan was listening so intently to us sharing our appreciation of him that many around the table were moved to tears. In that moment, the beauty and power of appreciation was so phenomenally powerful, even for a six-year-old. He was fully letting in our warmth and love shared verbally just for him. That's what feeling appreciation is all about.

PARENT DIRECTED

We doted on Angela as our firstborn when she was the only child in our home and we subscribed to a schedule to provide her with a regular routine. It helped her and us to have some reasonable semblance of a daily series of steps to follow. Mealtime, nap time, play time, bath time, story time, bedtime, etc., were daily activities within a daily routine that helped create balance for our family.

Of course, when Andrew arrived two and a half years later, a challenge to our beauty and order was presented. Adding children can add chaos to homes. Even young ones tend to have their own schedules and timings for things. And yet, we continued to seek a sense of gentle equilibrium within our home. We had to coordinate mealtimes and nap times between the two children. Of course, big sister wanted to be a big helper, and she was, at times. Differentiating between the needs of each child required a greater effort and diligence.

Aaron's arrival —before Angela turned five —meant yet another shift in our household management plan. While Angela was increasingly independent and able to take care of herself in certain ways, our ability to juggle the diverse needs of these three beautiful children was considerably challenging. Oftentimes, as one child was calm and being fed, another kid would be feeling emotional. And this chain of events could happen from time to time, including night time. A lot of time was spent comforting children to sleep during restless nights, which included rocking, singing, reading, listening. Yet we persevered in helping each of them to have a sense of stability no matter how each day unfolded.

We used strategies like winding down before bedtime, creating a regular evening routine which included showers, story time and discussing plans for tomorrow's activities. This helped create the order we talked about earlier. It's one of the reasons we have such admiration for single parents who may not have a natural person to take turns with during these activities. If that is the case, ask for help from those friends and family around you. It helps build community and preserves your sanity.

CREATING BEAUTY AND ORDER

In honoring one another and our children especially, we found ourselves creating beauty and order for Angela, Andrew, and Aaron. In other words, by helping create a dependable living situation and stable circumstances, individuals, children especially, are able to feel strong in foundation and better able to handle any difficulties that do come along. As parents, we sought to provide a home base and home life that gave our family a sense of security by meeting basic needs in order to give *all family members* greater personal capacity for academics, athletics, arts, socialization, etc.

Creating beauty in our home meant that we took time to clean up activities once we were done with them. Sometimes that meant that we picked up rooms or the house before bed time as a way to wind down. Pursuing beauty and order in our family felt very natural for us. We worked hard on regular routines, being physically active and having conversations about emotions and feelings.

We observed parents with a laid-back approach to parenting which meant that they didn't have schedules or routines that kept a tight hold on their homes. Laid-back parenting might work for some, letting children have more of a voice in their decisions and not impressing many rules or much structure. Every parent knows that flexibility is important in parenting, but at the same time, homes with no structure may create too much chaos to allow a child to thrive, and it may leave the parent feeling like a door mat.

Other parents were more dictatorial in their style. This means they abide by structure no matter what. Much like a drill sergeant, they have very little flexibility, and when things don't go as planned, they can not handle it well. It is their way or no way at all.

This led us in our curiosity to seek to understand more about the various parenting philosophies of our era.

ACTIVE PARENTS

The one authority that came to light in subsequent years was Dr. Michael Popkin, the founder of Active Parenting Inc. Dr. Popkin identified the extremes of parenting styles as either Autocratic or Permissive. His goal for parents was to find a place in the middle that he referred to as the Authoritative or Active Parenting style. The Active Parent allows the child increasing freedom as the child accepts more and more responsibility, in addition to respecting the rights of others.

We didn't know it at the time, but our goal was to become *Active Parents* who provided this freedom within expanding limits. The best example of our restrictive limits was the fact that we were typically the first family in the neighborhood, or one of the first, on any given evening to begin our bedtime routines, which started soon after dinner time. Sometimes this happened at holidays when cousins were present. At other times, it happened in our neighborhood when other kids were still outside and continuing to play. Our own kids weren't necessarily surprised, but not always happy, when we called them in on a summer evening because it was the appointed hour and time to get ready for bed. We were working to preserve a reasonable routine so that our kids woke up rested and refreshed the next day. Oftentimes, lack of sleep contributed to behavioral issues.

DISCIPLINE

When it came to discipline, we stayed away from actions that involved punishment. We chose to shift from the generations that relied on spanking, grounding, etc. for achieving behavioral changes to become more discipline focused. Askable parents choose a natural or logical consequence connected to the misbehavior.

Stepping back from a situation is really important in order to get the big picture. Removing a child from whatever is contributing to the behavior may also be an important step. Ultimately, we seek to use the opportunity as a teachable moment.

The word *discipline* is from the Latin word *disciplina* meaning "instruction and training." It's derived from the root word *discere*, which means "to learn." We sought to discipline or to teach, as opposed to punishment. With regard to behavior modification, our kids needed to know our limits for their behavior. The goal of disciplining was to share information and to teach by providing more information or context to the child for good decision-making.

Positive discipline connects consequences to the wayward action. If a plane is grounded, it loses mobility, the purpose for which it was created. When we ground a child, do we take all options away from them, even though the behavior has nothing to do with mobility? Consequences need to be either natural or logical. Connecting the discipline outcome to the original behavior if at all possible is desirable. For example, if I break someone's window, then I pay for the replacement and/or actually get involved in the purchase and the replacement process. That's logical.

Other misbehaviors result in natural consequences where spilling something at a meal or in the kitchen necessitates having the responsible party clean it up.

If a more serious misbehavior happens, then discipline, not punishment, is needed. As children get older, back talk or intentional refusal to accept parenting limits requires clear communication and appropriate transparency in order to re-set standards and expectations. It can be messy as kids test limits and seek increasing freedoms. As parents, we have a choice to implement the skills we're learning to work together as a family. That doesn't mean that we only intervene during misbehaviors.

GOOD CHOICES

We also worked to catch our kids making good choices. We acknowledged when they were supportive and helped things go well for our family. Early on, they understood that they were contributing to the good of all. By keeping positive, we were steering away from focusing on every little thing that they did *wrong*. The expression *where our attention flows, energy goes* fits here. If we dwell on everything that is not right, then we have little chance to pay attention to everything that is going well.

We also sought to keep from saying "ask your mom" or "ask your dad," realizing that that only set the kids up to exacerbate our conflict. Instead, as a couple, we often would choose to discuss the circumstances, weigh the evidence, and determine the next steps or consequences. We chose to be unified in order to not set the kids up to play us against one another. Of course, we didn't always agree, for example, when one of us wanted to prescribe tighter reins on an outing than the other thought was necessary. There came a point where we had built up sufficient trust in our parent/teen relationships that we had to acknowledge their right to independence and additional freedoms.

As parents, we had to intentionally seek to make decisions after looking at both sides of an issue, rather than out of fear. Our siblings, as well as our children, will tell you that we sometimes took time out from situations to discuss our next steps or remedies when a spur-of-the-moment reaction didn't fit the bill. Our discussions required ample conversation and dialogue. We were a good team, looking at both sides of issues, allowing us to be flexible and open with our kids. As much as possible, we tried to use good reasoning in our disciplining while focusing on logical and natural consequences.

NOT THE JONESES

In honoring our family, we spoke up when it was brought to our attention that some kids or families were not making the same choices we were making. Our response was usually something like, "well, we're not everybody else." We stood up for not conforming to all of the more popular trends, making decisions on what we valued as a family, not what others were choosing to do. We wanted the kids to understand that everyone makes choices, and they could do the same thing as they grew older. From our view, that worked out well.

We steered away from video games in our home. This meant that sometimes the kids found an opportunity to play in someone else's home. We were, however, among some of the first families to get a computer. We saw it as an educational tool that would serve our family well. And it did. It wasn't until our kids were older that we heard they had enjoyed not just our family computer for educational purposes but also for playing video games as well. Glad we got our money's worth out of it.

CHILD CENTERED

ROUTINE AND STRUCTURE

As we referenced near the beginning of this chapter, in our quest for beauty and order, we found tools to help in the success of the child. By providing family routine and structure, a parent provides a child with a reasonably repetitive pattern that is predictable. Spontaneity does have its place in offering opportunities for special treats, trips, or surprises to augment the family traditions that have been established. However, to be spontaneous all the time is no longer spontaneous; it can become a chaotic routine that provides little daily continuity.

A child coming home after school knows what the family expectations are upon arrival. That could be a check-in conversation with the parent, a snack from the refrigerator or a quiet time for reading. If predictability is difficult as to what a child will find at home, then they can be easily thrown off and possibly faced with unexpected hard choices that they may not be prepared to make.

The last several decades have seen an increasing percentage of children who return home with no adult present. The children come home alone, or with a sibling or two, until a parent or family member arrives to provide supervision. With proper preparation and communication, it is possible to provide routine and structure for children in these circumstances. A child coming home after school knows what family expectations are upon arrival, including securing the home and/or grabbing a snack from the refrigerator or a quiet time for centering.

We chose to have an adult available when the kids got home from school on most occasions. While that is just not possible for every family, creating the safest, most desirable circumstances possible must *consistently* be each parent's goal.

CHERISH

In the same way that a company tracks its bottom line in profits and losses, we were tracking our family's bottom line. We were seeking good results and optimum outcomes. In honoring our family, we first began by seeking to cherish our children. While there might have been many ways to do so, we sought to recognize them as a stunning, exhilarating expression of DIVINE creation. This meant that we told them verbally specific things that we appreciated in each of them. "I love how hard you worked playing baseball today." Initially, they were wholly dependent on us for every source of nutrition and complete care. When we think back to when they were toddlers, we watched them taking their first steps and eventually growing to have a mind of their own. We could increasingly celebrate their growth and all that they could become.

We accepted the responsibility in these early years of giving them their roots. We chose to be intentional about the ways in which we parented their needs. We were hopeful that if we encouraged them via balanced, focused strategies, they would develop deep roots and a strong core that would prepare them for the opportunities that would lie ahead in their lives. We intended that they would fully flourish as they developed their branches and blossomed in steady growth through the years.

CLEAR EXPECTATIONS (TEEN YEARS)

When it came to the teen years and curfew, we were very direct in expressing our desires: either make it home on time or let us know if that isn't going to be possible for some reason. We chose to purchase one of the earliest cell phones, which was the size of a brick. In particular, it was for Angela, our first teen driver, so that she could call us from anywhere, and we would not be imagining her in an accident or some other kind of a predicament somewhere. The phone went a long way toward providing good understanding and no surprises!

By respecting our request for clarity in this area, our kids honored us, as parents, by following through in communicating in a timely manner when they were coming home later than had been agreed upon. As parents, asking our kids to be respectful of one another as a family, including our concern for their safety, helped them recognize our corporate concern and they were good about respecting that. Our familial mutuality kept us respectful of what each of us needed. As parents, rather than sitting up late, awake and worried, we had clarity with regards to both our kids' whereabouts and with good understanding as to how to handle any emergency that might develop.

SPORTS

Angela was fortunate enough to get to play an Arizona high school varsity basketball game in the Phoenix Suns arena during her senior year. It was a game they could've won, and Angela had one of her best games on the court. She finished the game, having worked hard while performing well. And while losing the game wasn't fun, she can be endlessly proud of her accomplishment on a team that came so very close to pinnacle performance.

Similarly, Aaron was a contributing member of an Arizona state championship track team in his junior year in high school. In his senior year, the opportunity to possibly exceed junior year accomplishments was not to be. Late in the season, he suffered a stress fracture in his foot which made it impossible to compete. . . although he tried. He had feelings of disappointment; however, he could rest in the knowledge that he had done his best and made contributions when able, and he made great friendships.

Doing one's best is of utmost priority. Finding joy in our effort is also important. And when it comes to performance, being a good sport is equally significant. Work hard. Have fun. Be a good sport. Cherish your teammates. Respect your fellow competitors. Striving for personal best is all that is asked. Helping each child feel their own pride in their effort and enjoyment will help them go far.

Tools to Plan: We intentionally sought to provide a stable daily schedule so that our kids could depend on a consistent daily routine. Even though change is a reality in the developmental progress of a child, we were seriously intentional in framing our parenting efforts by balancing structure and flexibility. We didn't skip meals. While we learned the term *hangry* later in life, we knew that a hungry kid wasn't always a very cooperative one. So we tried to stay ahead of nutritional needs by meal planning which was timed to be ready to eat *before* hangry happened.

Another strategy we employed centered around intentionally preparing for tomorrow. It helped to review the plans ahead and get specific as we approached outings. We shared information about how long we would be involved or what time we would be home and asked for cooperation in helping to prepare our kids for the upcoming event. As parents we did our best to keep to the framework and not stretch anyone's patience.

By providing day-to-day clarity, we tried to head off misunderstandings that often arise when kids find themselves in situations which they were not prepared for. We sought to teach and inform first. Obviously, not everything went exactly as planned or as we might have expected. Anticipating kids' needs was on top of our priority list so they had some ownership of the time frame of activities to which we were committed.

Here is a checklist to think about as you make a consistent daily routine, schedules, and build in clarity for your family:

1. Do you have a way to make sure everyone eats every three to four hours to avoid hangry (hungry/angry) issues?
2. Do events on the calendar have rides and time to get there?
3. Does everyone know the daily and weekly schedule?
4. Do all the students in the family have supplies for their weekly school work?

5. Is all the technology updated and ready to be utilized for school?
6. What community and social activities are on our calendar and do any of them conflict?

TOOLS

Calm before bed: We usually took time to help the kids settle in for the night by reading to them and/or listening to them talk about their day. And often, it included giving the kids good information about what tomorrow's schedule was going to look like, in case it was anything out of the ordinary. Some who have known us over the years know that clarity was paramount in our family which helped us smooth out expectations and give our kids the ability to joyfully anticipate tomorrow

Settle the Day: We did take the strategy of spending time with them after the common evening routine: bath/shower, reading, and after a bedtime prayer, to help them *settle the day*. Being able to listen to them share what they needed was our means of letting them know they were loved and accepted. We often practiced Good Touch by rubbing their feet to help soothe and quiet them for rest.

Purposeful workspace: The *beauty and order* that can be created in the home extends to the hardships of the house itself. Declaring a certain room or space or table as the 'homework center' can be clarifying for children. Providing essential supplies, music options, etc., will help develop the proper mindset and expectations for successful effort at home and expectation for success in the classroom. Giving sufficient attention to beauty and order can pay huge dividends year in and year out so that every family member feels honored and secure.

Active Listening: In seeking clarity and understanding, when it comes to communication, we fully recognized the importance of doing more than hearing one another. Rather, we did our best to really listen to one another. Over the years, we've learned a lot about the difference between *hearing* and *listening*. That means seeking to understand the context, the perspective and allowing space for full expression. Sometimes such communication was just reporting. Sometimes it was sharing hurts or anger. Listening is an honoring activity. Listening to the voices of children in our homes means giving children opportunities to express themselves. Best results are achieved through intentional communication strategies in which family members prioritize time with one another.

The Timer: In reflecting on both hearing and listening, if there was one strategy that paid the biggest dividends over time, it was our use of the kitchen timer. At mealtime, a timer can be used to provide each person with a set amount of time to share about their day.

In ensuring good communication and helping the family unit to work well, the use of a timer in order to give each family member a turn to talk, share, or celebrate promotes inclusivity and a balance of power. We used it extensively, and still do.

A timer provides a ground rule for sharing. Each person gets equal time to speak. Others are expected to listen when they are not sharing. At mealtime, a timer can be used to provide each person with two to three minutes each to tell about their day, or to express what they are looking forward to. If utilized in a family meeting, each person can have one minute to make suggestions toward resolution of a family issue that needs creative thinking to solve.

In our family, sharing time meant using the timer as mentioned earlier and giving everyone, including guests and friends present, the chance to participate however they desired. In the case of our family, we were in multiple schools with each of us having different experiences. It was extra important to hear how every family member was doing.

Without the timer, there is the risk that the conversation will center on only one or two family members, leaving others to listen without talking. Of course, while the timer is probably best utilized at mealtime, it does not have to be used at every meal. The joy of family conversation cannot be scripted. The use of time shared equally on a regular basis, however, helps families listen to the voices of all, not just a few.

The timer provided a structure for hearing one another. More than hearing, we were working on listening to each other in order to understand. As parents, we derived information that helped us process as a couple if there was an intervention of some sort needed in one of the kid's situations. To listen is to honor. It builds respect. It fosters trust. It proves we care. One great-grandmother remarked: "If we had employed the timer at our dinner table, our youngest would have been able to overcome his stuttering. At mealtime, with three older sisters and parents surrounding him, he could hardly get a word in edgewise."

When to turn off the timer: Not all communication is clean and sweet. A timer may not always be useful or needed. Sometimes we participated in conversation as participants with a family member as a mediator, helping two family members work things out. Sometimes a timer worked really well in these circumstances to keep one from interrupting another and reminding all to listen and take turns.

Know when to say yes and when to say no: It took specific parenting actions to create the right foundation for our kids. Keeping that balance was important to us also. Managing a family of five automatically generates a lot of give and take. A lot of monitoring and adjusting.

For example, with various commitments, conflicting game/activity times meant John going one direction while Deborah went another. We often talked about getting on the same page in our parenting. How could we keep equilibrium if we were going in opposite directions or had major differences in philosophy?

How we adapt as parents, recognizing the changes underway as well as these varying needs definitely keeps us on our toes. We knew that with every developmental stage, we were responsible for creating a zest for living and learning, a resilience for the challenges ahead, and yet a peace of mind for them that allowed them to rest assured that *everything would be all right* in the days, weeks, months, and years ahead. We were seeking to be proactive in the short term for the long-term outcomes we sought for the family!

Words matter: How much honoring is expressed and cemented in the three words: *I love you.* Isn't it fascinating how we can be *frustrated* by the smallest little behaviors of our children? We tend to zero in on what annoys us, and we let them know about it. Instead of reassuring them of our love for them, we derail and fail to give kudos and share love as we obviously know would be better for them.

We sought to say *I love you* regularly, and occasionally, we put it in writing via a written note. We could have expressed *I love you* way more, and we encourage those of you reading this to keep expressing your love. Not only does it help reinforce the family love we are seeking to instill but it also lets children know that their parents, and their Divine Creator, care about them.

Healthy touch: Over the years, we chose positive physical touch in our interactions with our kids. It was another modality to express love to our family. And we derived a similar benefit also. We chose to share warmth and expressions of physical caring for the huge benefits it gave to them. Hugs were a pretty normal action around our house. As parents, when they were young, we liked getting down on our knees to get on their level to share a hug as the situation dictated. Beyond hugging, we also made an effort to just be present!

You've already read about foot rubbing in our bedtime routine. We chose to normalize physical touch in our family for the affirmation it provided and largely to acknowledge and make other family members feel supported. We also gave high fives, low fives, chest bumps, etc.

We knew TV watching could be both beneficial and detrimental at the same time. We liked sitting on the couch or on the floor next to the kids to watch with them and to be physically in touch. During commercials, we might interject about the previous segment, either to ask a question or check for understanding. This also helped the kids from *zoning out* and kept their brains alert and aware. Without a doubt, both Sesame Street and Mr. Rogers' Neighborhood were our two favorite, and most frequently watched, kids' shows. And it was helpful that Mr. Rogers was outspoken about the importance of hugs.

Power of self praise: And at least partially in Mr. Rogers' spirit, in our parenting, we were in the habit of telling our kids: "If I were you, I'd be proud of myself." It was suggested to us that by telling them, "We're proud of you," makes their efforts more about performing for us than for themselves. We sought to transfer the pride of individual performance or personal accomplishment onto their shoulders, not ours.

We also stressed the phrase "work hard and have fun. . ." as we sought for them to both give their best effort while seeking to find the fun in their effort. Ultimately, in life, they will own their efforts and significance for their own joy and pleasure, not for ours. Helping each child take ownership of their accomplishments and not performing for someone else was our goal.

CLOSING

Here are several borrowed concepts that seem to have paid the highest dividends through the years. Honoring encompasses so many elements.

As a family, we learned these tips from watching Mr. Rogers:

1. It's OK to feel whatever it is that we feel, but not an excuse for bad behavior.
2. Other people are different from us, and just as complex as we are.
3. We can work to make a difference right where we are.
4. It's important to make time to care for ourselves.

Like Mr. Rogers, we found parenting most successful when we shifted into a child-centered or child-focused parenting style. This does not mean over focusing on our children while ignoring our own needs. Rather, it means paying attention as parents to the needs of our children, both short term and long term. Every parent knows it is easy to be distracted, especially these days with social media and screen time occupying so much of our attention. Staying present, in the moment, with our children tells our kids how important they are to us and helps them to thrive.

With the complexity of our adult lives as we circulate in the many networks of home, work, friends, faith-based community, and all other interests calling out our energy. . . it can be difficult to keep our kids front and center in our lives. Reminding ourselves that they will only have a relatively brief number of years with us. . . before friends and future endeavors begin to draw their attention. . . we must choose to make sure they know that they are at the top of our life priority list.

While interruptions will pop up and get in the way, clearing the way for our kids first will help cement our relationships with them and build trust among our family for the long haul.

We chose to show up at school by attending, participating, volunteering, etc. Same is true with regard to friends and social groups. We also chose to be present so that we rarely missed these special moments.

REFLECTION QUESTIONS

1. What types of conscious consequences do you give your kids when they make mistakes?

   _____

   _____

   _____

   _____

2. What listening strategies do you employ so that all of the family members feel heard?

   _____

   _____

   _____

   _____

3. How would you use the phrase, "if I were you, I'd be proud of . . ." with your children?

_____

_____

_____

_____

4. What structure helps you with consistency in your home? What would you like to implement?

_____

_____

_____

_____

5.   What's the best way to use physical touch to make your family feel healthy and cared for?

_____

_____

_____

_____

CHAPTER 3

BROKENNESS

"We embrace movement from past or current brokenness in developing strength of character."

As we look back over the years: when we were children, while we were parenting, and today, as we are still learning as grandparents. . . some of the life challenges we've experienced have meant personal hurts that have led to brokenness.

As we all know, brokenness is part of life's fabric. While no one wants to live in brokenness, it is impossible not to face setbacks in life. Stuff happens. And we figure out not everything is under our control. What we do control is how we respond when things do not go the ways we'd like them to.

We feel it's important in setbacks of any kind to seek to see the big picture in order to better understand what is contributing to it. And we need to keep from self sabotaging through the process. We might feel inclined to blame someone else. We might rationalize or excuse the incident as out of our control. Ultimately, on the parenting journey, children push us to examine our own personal issues, including the questions:

1. What life challenges am I facing today?
2. What was it like in my own growing up years?
3. How was I parented? What did I experience?
4. What did I have to overcome in my life journey?

If we get challenged and just throw up our hands and yield to brokenness and accept it as the norm, we lose the opportunity to make a situation better. We also miss the chance to teach a life lesson to our children and/or learn a lesson ourselves. Of course, if we own a car and it has a flat tire or a bad battery, we take steps to fix those problems. It's logical and practical. As we parent, not everything is perfectly logical nor practical.

By analyzing the origin of the brokenness and working to find success in living with the conflict or shortcoming, we take the next step in parenting. It's a lot like needing to get our car back on the road. First, we analyze. What needs to be done in our brokenness to get our vehicle back on the road or to make the family whole again? Once we're back up and running, how do we maintain that standard? What are the steps to regular maintenance via thinking ahead and working ahead that will help us head off brokenness? Staying faithful to the little things, responding to difficulties, and persevering will get us to our intended destination.

PARENT DIRECTED

Examining our own issues helps to assure the car keeps running. As adults, we have to be honest about our personal issues. It can mean checking ourselves to assure we are feeling satisfied in our occupational or career journeys. Are there goals or dreams that we choose to pursue? What long-term outcomes are we seeking?

Self-examination is key.

1. Am I reading into an issue through the lens of my own childhood? How is this situation the same or different than when I experienced it?

---

2. What feelings most accurately express what is going on inside of me?

_____

_____

_____

_____

3. How can I show up for my child in a way my own parent(s) may or may not have shown up for me?

_____

_____

_____

_____

4.   If I were in the same situation, how would I want it handled at an age-appropriate level?

_____

_____

_____

_____

5.   Think about the adult child you want to have. . . what characteristics do they possess? Is there a way to deal with the current situation that allows them to learn those same characteristics?

_____

_____

_____

_____

GRIEF AND LOSS

Losses happen throughout our lives. Some develop over time. Some happen suddenly. While it took a number of years to come to full realization of a major factor in her upbringing, Deborah's self-examination helped her discover one of the biggest factors in how she was parented. At the age of four, Deborah's family experienced a major loss with the tragic death of her aunt and her uncle.

In her growing-up years, she observed and experienced family pain over the holidays. During extended family gatherings, collective family grief was shared over the loss of her aunt and her husband in the extended family. Deborah witnessed this shared grief as expressed in words and tears as family gathered at Christmas or Easter, in remembering these two precious members.

In this pain and hurt, with no formal grief counseling, Deborah felt that her parents raised her with lots of protective boundaries. They did their best; however, their unhealthy fear complicated by their unresolved grief meant lots of restrictions to hopefully prevent any similar tragedy to ever take place.

Beginning in college, Deborah began a journey that she could not have anticipated. She had moved away from her home community and was a sponge, soaking up all the world had to offer her at Manchester College. Introduction to Psychology invited her into a consciousness of thought that has continued to this day.

In Deborah's grief and loss journey, she recognized that she sometimes made parenting decisions based on unhealthy fear.

Her vulnerability with her children allowed her to discern and be more open-minded in her decision-making.

As Deborah grew older, it brought a lot of peace to her heart to be able to ask questions and to have conversations with her grandparents as they shared memories and voiced feelings about their own losses. While Deborah and John were in the throes of parenting, Deborah recognized that some of her parenting choices were fear based and sometimes connected to this family tragedy.

Without question, the way a family experiences a tragedy or loss will affect the family dynamics. Deborah chose to engage grief and loss by seeking more skills and tools with attending workshops, reading, and taking positive action in order to change up her generational blueprint. Our experiences led us to deeper understandings about the importance of processing grief and loss.

We all come to grief and loss with varying perspectives. It is commonly understood that any kind of tragedy or loss can leave a mark on our lives. There is no question that acknowledging brokenness is important in the overall health of each family. Sometimes the loss, hurt, or disappointment happens during our growing-up years. And sometimes our greatest losses happen well into adulthood. Either way, when it happens, it can often blind side you.

BAD TOUCH

We valued and practiced good touch within our family and among our friends. We sought intentional touching of our children to express good vibes among our family. Hugs and warm touches, like back rubs or just sitting next to one another on the couch, were part of the standard operating procedures in our family. In that context, we were blindsided in learning about what happened to Aaron.

Aaron was the youngest in our neighborhood. On a regular basis, Andy and Aaron enjoyed playing with neighborhood boys, on our street there were actually many kids, fairly close in age. Sometimes it was baseball, other times soccer, or football, or hide and seek. These children played long hours quite successfully while being good sports.

However, we learned that over a short period one summer, one neighbor boy was influencing Aaron to participate in sexual touch. We were disappointed that Aaron had been so affected and we felt angry and hurt when we heard the story from his brother.

We chose for John to speak with the father of the boy. John reported what we understood had happened and shared our concern. The father said it seemed fairly harmless to him, as kids do funny things sometimes, but he would take care of it with his boy, with the understanding it wouldn't happen again. We shared our deep love and empathy with Aaron by keeping the door open for him to share with us as he worked through his feelings of hurt and shame.

Today, we more fully recognize that Aaron's perception was and is different from our parental perception. We consider it important to honor his journey. As we look back, we would take proactive steps today in pursuing interventions and counseling opportunities that we didn't take then. At the time, we did the best we could with the information we had at hand. We applaud Aaron as he has chosen wholeness in healing through this experience on his lifelong wellness journey.

We know that we have choices when brokenness happens. We can choose health, healing and closure. This is a response that we want to be our initial reaction when something happens; however, oftentimes, it is one of hiding, retreating and even shame. We are worried that we made the wrong decision or we think we may make a wrong one later. We want to choose health, but we aren't sure where to start. It can confuse us and our families.

Even worse, brokenness of any kind can breed fear in a family. It can lead to unhealthy drama and disrupt the best intended communication. We make healthy choices if we listen to one another, share honestly in sensitive ways, and then seek understanding for the sake of family clarity. How we undertake our own work at awareness is important. Discerning the difference between healthy and unhealthy fear takes time and effort. Therapy can help us dive deeper and develop a greater understanding of what's behind our tendencies or behaviors.

Unless we forge new parenting paths, we will likely resort back to how we were parented. That may or may not be helpful to our own children. Again, intentionality helps us to declare our strategies for our parenting direction and helps us to honor yet retreat from those methods that we found most unacceptable as utilized in how we were parented.

In the need for parents to examine themselves, Steven Covey, educator and author, expresses so well what we have come to appreciate for overcoming problems and creating solutions when he writes:

> "*When parents see their children's problems as opportunities to build the relationship instead of as negative, burdensome irritations, it totally changes the nature of parent-child interaction. Parents become more willing, even excited, about deeply understanding and helping their children. When a child comes to a parent with a problem, instead of thinking, 'Oh no! Not another problem!' their paradigm is, 'Here is a great opportunity for me to really help my child and to invest in our relationship.'*"
>
> Covey writes: "*Many interactions change from transactional to transformational, and strong bonds of love and trust are created as children sense the value parents give to their problems and to them as individuals.*"

In seeking to better understand ourselves, we strived to turn our kids' situations from a problem to an opportunity. We often said we hoped our kids would take the best of each of us into adulthood. That means we hoped they would take what served them well and build on that foundation. At the same time, you can't have a good foundation without advance planning. That advance planning can lead to new paths, new careers and even new homes.

CHILD CENTERED

In our early thirties, we were setting our sights on new career paths. And since we'd already successfully navigated previous career changes, we weren't afraid to take some risks. As it turned out, the best opportunities we found were readily available in Arizona.

When we made our decision to leave Indiana and move to Arizona, we knew that Andy, our eldest son, was very sad about leaving Indiana. He was very comfortable with friends in the neighborhood, a school just two blocks away, and grandparents loving on him. We listened to him and let him share his hurt and angry feelings. We had tearful goodbyes with friends and family. We talked about our fears as we identified the unknowns that were ahead. As we prepared for the journey, Andy could see we were trusting God to show us the way.

During the first few years in Arizona, we continued to honor Andy's need to vent his frustrations. He needed to process his grief in order to take positive steps into his new community. In Arizona, he became more and more comfortable with his surroundings, making friends in the neighborhood, and enjoying his new school.

Through the years, he was ecstatic about our summer road trips back to the Midwest and became chief navigator every time, predicting arrival times, when and where to get gas, have lunch, etc. He also prearranged time with his friends back in Indiana as he sought to maintain and rekindle those relationships. To this day, while living in Arizona, he has maintained friendships with a number of his original Indiana childhood friends.

Parenting has a way of exposing us. There is transparency whether we like it or not. While Andy accepted that we were the adults and therefore got to make the decisions, that didn't mean he had to like them. As parents, there's nowhere to hide. Taking stock of our own issues, insecurities, or shortcomings can be revealing. Each parent brings a blueprint to the table. This blueprint includes all the experiences that have happened through the years to influence how we tackle the challenging, yet ultimately rewarding responsibility of being a parent.

While Andy's lament about our family's geographical move was handled mostly by listening to him and allowing him to express his hurts, fears, and even tears…there are situations that call for parent interventions of a more action-based approach. Andy didn't misbehave. He expressed his disappointment fully.

If his frustration had resulted in acting out by becoming overtly aggressive or disrespectful, we would have needed to find another approach to managing the situation. Through the years, parents have taken many different views of behavior modification.

GENERATIONAL CHANGES

We chose to shift from the generation that relied on punishment by way of spanking, grounding, etc. for achieving behavioral changes, to become more discipline focused. We centered on choosing a natural or logical consequence connected to the mis-behavior. We were introduced to this approach from Rudolph Dreikurs, especially his work *Children the Challenge*. Stepping back from a situation is really important in order to get the big picture. Removing a child from whatever is contributing to the behavior may also be an important step. Ultimately, we seek to use the opportunity as a teachable moment.

When disciplining, consequences needed to be extended. That sometimes meant we had to live with the burden it pre-sented. For example, if we were looking forward to an outing of some sort, but a behavior had made such a trip impossible, that meant no one was going anywhere. Not only did the child face the consequence, but now we, as parents, had consequenc-es to deal with as well.

We have been in the grocery store with a partially filled bas-ket when one or more of the kids were just not in the right space to finish our shopping. In at least one case, we left the store and the shopping cart behind. That was a consequence that was logical, although as the parents we didn't get done what we had expected to accomplish.

Other misbehaviors result in natural consequences where spilling something at a meal or in the kitchen necessitates having the responsible party clean up the mess they made. If a more serious misbehavior happens, then discipline, not punishment is needed. As children get older, back talk or intentional refusal to accept parenting limits requires clear communication and appropriate transparency in order to re-set standards and expectations. It can be messy as kids test limits and seek increasing freedoms. As parents, we have a choice to implement the skills we're learning to work together as a family.

POSITIVE STEPS

Intentionality has been of utmost importance in our parenting development. While parenting can occur just by happenstance, we prefer to believe that taking an intentional path to outcomes is exceedingly important. The adage *an ounce of prevention is worth a pound of cure* fits here. Rather than rearing a child while just hoping for the best, why not take positive steps to ensure their physical safety, emotional maturation, and confidence in their ability to make healthy day to day decisions and bigger life choices too.

We found it a good idea to work closely with children from a young age so that their path was smoother as they got older. That, of course, didn't work in all areas, but we wanted there to be less of a risk if we guided them well earlier. By taking intentional steps along the way, a great deal of heartache can be avoided, and a child can be better launched into a meaningful, balanced, and successful life journey.

A couple of generations ago, a common phrase often repeated was: "Children are to be seen; not heard." This adage was one that pushed the agenda of children having less value. They didn't need to talk, because they didn't have important things to say. We know today that this is far from true. Our kids have very valuable things to say, which is why listening with our timer was such a crucial part of our parenting.

We more fully realize the importance of giving a child the best opportunity to feel loved, honored, listened to and respected. By doing so, a parent or an educator expresses a mutual respect for a child and encourages the child to launch him or herself into learning and growing with both energy and enthusiasm.

Giving our children the opportunity to feel loved even when going through brokenness or grief can help reinforce the notion that hard things should bring us together instead of pulling us apart. These hard things are our hard things to experience and grow through regardless of the size of that struggle.

We know grief does not just involve leaving a hometown or actual loss of a loved one. We know grief can surround any and all personal losses. As kids, it can happen when a good friend moves away or goes to a different school. And other times it happens in adult relationships. Spouses and partners break up.

Such was the case for our daughter, Angela. When she was in the midst of couple conflict, including marital counseling, separation, and eventually divorce, it meant that our family was affected. Over a couple of years, each of us were listeners to her and obviously cared deeply for her and our grandchildren's wellbeing in the course of the family splintering. Sometimes we were directly involved in trying to find resolution between them. While it was her journey, we sought to be present for her and help her process her choices in the matter. We felt considerable sympathy and love, knowing how hard she was working to find resolution in the brokenness.

Between John's dad's death in September of 2010 and Deborah's father's passing in July of 2011, our grief and loss were magnified. These losses coincided with Angela's divorce journey, and we all had a lot to overcome in order to persevere through our complexity of feelings.

On top of these losses, and while our family was grieving, we were in the midst of sponsoring Health, Balance, Leadership Teen Camp in Prescott, AZ. During our camp planning, we would share in our grief and even questioned whether we were able to carry out the camp responsibilities. While we knew that planning and putting on a camp wouldn't fix our grief, sharing it with each other during our planning sessions brought us all closer together as a family. We knew that there were teens across our city that had grief, as well, and didn't have the resources and families to provide those spaces for them to grow from it. So we proceeded to invite and host our camp. Thankfully, we were able to hold space for one another and successfully directed our camp for a number of students, some of whom we are still connected with today.

When we look back over the years, we recognize that supporting Angela to emerge from divorce was one of the most challenging times our family ever dealt with. Watching as she found her power and regained her footing was emotionally difficult. Through those times, each family member was walking with Angela in her situation while dealing with our own grief and loss in the passing of our fathers and grandfathers, respectively. Angela had to call on all of her courage to put the past behind her and rally to a new paradigm.

We have watched her handle the adversity and find independence again. We are proud of who she has become. We find it exceedingly important to let our children know it is OK to be proud of themselves, especially when emerging from brokenness.

COMMUNITY SUPPORTED

COMMUNICATION IS KEY

Do you ever think about how we learn to communicate? Is it not absolutely clear that we learn communication from those who raise us?

As adults, when we say that we are most abundantly influenced by the five people we spend the most time with. . . can we not extrapolate that the same is true with regard to who parented us? Who were the five most significant influencers of our communication skills and style: A Parent? Extended family member? Neighbor? Teacher?

Probably the single most complex issue with family brokenness stems from our communication. Sometimes we say things that are unkind or upsetting to the one receiving our words. Brokenness happens when we are not clear and yet we are expecting others to anticipate or understand what we choose to share. That is a formula for misunderstanding and hurt.

Finding our way through miscommunication is something of a lifetime endeavor. From one day to the next, we can go from being on the same page to not even close to being in the same book. We stumble and bumble through our feelings, through rash statements, through a poor choice of words, etc., and our communication within the family breaks down.

Sometimes what we don't say can be even more complicated. Especially if we *assume* that what we desire *should* be understood without any words being spoken. Passive behaviors ignore issues and may work for a while, but eventually, and usually, will emerge in other ways. Being proactive and forthcoming with regard to managing family communication issues is critical to a balanced and productive family.

When friends or extended family members young and old passed away, our children needed to be comforted and informed. While we were processing our own grief, it was important to pay attention to our children. Taking time with our children to listen to their fears and hurts was important. Or just answering their questions to the best of our ability.

Here again, we had to remind ourselves that we were taking short-term actions for long-term gains and purposes. Within the first two years of moving to Arizona, a neighbor boy down our street was struck by a vehicle and eventually died. We remember kneeling down and holding our boys at our front door and praying for this family shortly after the accident. If we use moments like this one to provide clarity and understanding, our children will be better served as they move forward through life. Seeking to be honest is important within the context of the child's age and ability to understand. Being conscientious and discerning is most important in the context of a parent's honesty. This looks unique according to your family's current needs.

DIFFERENT FAMILIES, DIFFERENT NEEDS

During our school counseling careers, we served hundreds of students and families through both joyous and difficult times. We saw the best of kids and families and we saw some of the worst situations imaginable. We provided crisis intervention, both on an individual basis and on a school-by-school basis as needed. It would seem we saw almost every imaginable family circumstance; again, some in celebration and others in complete sorrow or dysfunction.

In working with colleagues and administrators, we found the most successful parenting intervention strategies happened when parents were curious, involved, and transparent. When they came to us with issues and allowed us to help them seek problem-solving solutions, good outcomes were found. Occasionally we referred families to outside agencies when it was vital that the entire family be involved in working toward solutions.

Understandably, all of our professional training and seat-of-the-pants experiences lent themselves to practicing holistic parenting in our own family. If you've ever watched a Fire Department or EMT crew respond to any emergency situation, then you know how cool and calm they seem. And yet every situation they encounter is unlike any before. As a family we have to stay as settled and collected as possible and handle each encounter creatively. And we better understand that we never know exactly what tomorrow will bring our way. Sometimes it was necessary to get together as a couple alone to 'discuss' next steps when an unexpected issue came our way like when one of the kids wanted permission to go somewhere and we needed to decide yes or no and render a collective verdict.

In the early '80s, we were reading books we liked to help build trust and love in our family and to raise happier, healthier children. We were in our mid to late twenties when our kids were born. We expected we had enough life experience to help us carry out our parental responsibilities. Lo and behold, we found out that the journey was going to require us to sacrifice. . . way more than we thought might be necessary. The reality was, yes, we had some information, but on the other hand, we had a long way to go. Many authors made it clear that raising children would require a lot from us.

TOOLS

Our various stories of adversity differ, and admittedly, each of us felt frustration and disappointment through it all. At any time, we could have become hopeless and discouraged enough to give up our plans. . . but we kept an upward trajectory and persevered. The greatest lessons learned from our various and challenging childhood episodes was the fundamental belief that anything could be overcome. It was the fact that we took an optimist's attitude rather than the pessimist's downward spiral. Baby steps in perseverance made all the difference. Being committed to recognizing the disappointment, and in spite of the difficulty, moving forward anyway.

What are the best steps towards intentionally parenting well? Let's begin with taking care of ourselves. Think of this as we do when the flight attendant reminds us to put the oxygen mask on ourselves first before securing our child's mask. If we are paying attention to our own needs, then we are better able to be mindful of our children's needs.

Balance: Of course, this varies from individual to individual and family to family. Examine how well you are balancing your parenting with the other demands and needs for your time and attention. By paying attention to our personal status, we can choose a course of action to better balance our needs with the family needs.

Our couple's love was expressed in our common purpose as partners and as parents. We were united in support of one another and our children. We frequently took walks together to get outside, get fresh air, debrief our days, and process past, present, and future.

Self Care: This might seem unusual to express, but perhaps the best step we took in self-care for ourselves and for our family was the purchase of our first timeshare property, not long after arriving in Arizona. That purchase turned out to be a timely decision for us. It propelled us to places we might have only dreamed about. Up to that point, with rare exception, the extent of our vacations was road trips to the Midwest to visit our families in the summer.

Our timeshare exchanges took our family to a variety of stateside visits to Utah, California, Colorado, and Virginia. We got to see other parts of the country and meet other vacationers, while giving us more family time to hike, swim, travel, and play together. We even made property exchanges into England and Spain when Andy & Aaron were on college semesters abroad.

Talk about the hard stuff: Sometimes within a family, we have differences of opinion. Of course, we do. We're different human beings, each of us doing our best to make sense of our world. By the way, we believe it is all right to have differences of opinion. Especially between parent(s) and children. We are vastly different, particularly with regard to the eras in which we grew up/are growing up. Perceptions are different for lots of reasons.

Being able to express those different views is important in a healthy family. When we encounter such differences, the timer strategy from our previous chapter may be particularly useful as each family member shares time by expressing their views without interruption. While we might end up agreeing to disagree, consensus can also be reached in this way. It does take diligence in listening to one another and allowing time to fully develop the discussion.

I Apologize: When am I sorry? When do I apologize? How do I learn from my mistakes? How do I offer sincere condolences when my choice, words, action, or inaction is hurtful or harmful to someone else? When am I willing to come off of my *I'm the best* pedestal and really face the facts? Are we going to be the one to offer the olive branch of reconciliation? As so many of us already know, that is very difficult to do. Saying *I apologize* is both challenging and humbling at the same time.

Be Transparent: A healthy fear normally incorporates greater transparency to better generate understanding. Healthy fear can be informative and can protect us or provide safety. It also requires us to recognize it. As parents, we need to be aware of any displaced feelings that generate less gratefulness and behaviors that are more knee-jerk than necessary. When young people have ideas, a parent's responsibility is to listen. Listen to their rationales; listen to their sense of purpose; listen to seek understanding. Seek a compromise, if available, and find guidance if it is desired.

Practice Communication: Brokenness is likely to happen when there is a breakdown in communication. Communication is transformational. It's both a function of what we *do* say, as well as what we *don't* say. Seeking to create mastery in communication will go a long way toward heading off parenting problems. Transparency for clarity moves a family forward in positive communication and holistic understanding. Coming to parenting with an open mind by asking questions and seeking transparency can create a healthy dynamic.

Lifetime learning has become a household word these days. Never give up. Keep learning! As parents, if we think we can just *hold our breath* from the time the kids arrive until the kids leave the nest. . . well, we'd obviously run out of oxygen first. Better to 'take a deep breath' and dive into the challenges, seek mutuality and daily learning opportunities.

CLOSING

FORGIVENESS

Forgiveness can be a challenging process for school-age kids. Admittedly, it can be difficult for adults as well. As school counselors, we helped students walk through their forgiveness journeys. Because our counseling duties involved some interventions, we had various opportunities to help kids get clear and move forward, to the best of our abilities. That didn't mean that they were done with brokenness, but it was a chance to give them tools when future issues showed up.

Forgiving each other and forgiving ourselves is vital if we are going to help our family through the brokenness journey. A key component of forgiveness is knowing the issue at hand. Being able to look at it, talk about it and feel it can start the healing process. Our faith journey helped us target the wounds that needed to be dealt with and not ignored. We have seen the power of outside resources like therapy, coaches and people to lean on. The effects of these to the recipient helps the individual make incredible strides towards healing. Oftentimes, we need someone else to walk through it with us since we are too close inside the brokenness to see things clearly.

Forgiveness does not happen overnight. Being able to release disappointment and frustration is important soul work. It's important in the recovery process. It's a long-term process. It may never be done, but that work is still worth it. It doesn't happen by just snapping your fingers. There's no magic involved. Just like hiking a mountain, we don't often see the end result in the beginning; however, after we continually take one step in front of the other, we get there. We get to the top. And we get to the healing, we get through the brokenness one step at a time.

We as a family know that we will never be free from brokenness, but with our healing process, we get closer to freedom.

We also don't have to let brokenness define us or our family and relationships.

The opportunity that brokenness offers us is the understanding that although life will hand us setbacks, we can overcome them. Living into brokenness means accepting that it is part of life. If we choose to ignore brokenness, we can be sure it will stay with us in various ways and show back up in our lives until we choose to deal with it.

Loving ourselves through brokenness keeps us growing. In his book *Encouraging Children to Learn*, Rudolf Dreikurs wrote: "A child needs encouragement like a plant needs water." Knowing that brokenness is a given requires us to stay encouraging for ourselves and especially for our children. Seeking transformation through brokenness will bring us to breakthroughs and success.

Brokenness can be so difficult that we may think of giving up. But do we stop driving when our car breaks down? Do we just junk that car? No. And we challenge you that we don't and we shouldn't. In life, like the vehicle, we have to repair the damage, regain confidence, and keep on driving down the road of life. If we just remain parked in the driveway, we will miss all the amazing places this journey is intended to take us.

REFLECTION QUESTIONS

1. What are three things that you thought were good about the way you were parented growing up? What three things would you change?

   _____

   _____

   _____

   _____

2. What sorts of fears have been showing up in your parenting? How have they influenced your decisions?

   _____

   _____

   _____

   _____

3. Are there ways you can be transparent in your parenting while listening and giving guidance?

_____

_____

_____

_____

4. What things did you experience growing up that impact your parenting now?

_____

_____

_____

_____

5. What are three ways you plan to work on the brokenness that shows up in life?

_____

_____

_____

_____

CHAPTER 4

ENTREPRENEURIAL SPIRIT

"Together we faithfully invested time and resources with vision to create pathways to unlimited opportunities."

There is a connection between building a family and building a business. Now that we have built both we see the resiliency that parents and owners need to have. Launching a successful family requires stamina and persistence. These same attributes will aid a fledgling business to succeed when they first experience hardships and challenges.

Whether building a family or building a business we need to be intentional. Do you believe life just happens to us or do we choose our outcomes? Do you feel life is like the proverbial ping pong ball that just bounces and bounces all over the place until the laws of physics bring it to rest?

If our life is like a ping pong ball, then we accept that life is a series of getting knocked around by careers, bills, school, etc. Instead, we must believe that what takes place in our lives and what comes along in our journey is a direct reflection of our own choices.

In a 2018 study titled, *Autopilot Britain* by Marks and Spenser, of 3,000 individuals surveyed, 96 percent reported living on autopilot. The researchers concluded that as our lives have become more frantic and the needle has moved ever more toward the 'overwhelm,' autopilot has become our default mode. When we default to autopilot, we feel extra stress, anxiety, and fear of the unknown.

Autopilot makes us think of airline pilots, or more recently, we can purchase vehicles that are self-driving. For us, we chose to ride bikes a lot as a family. John chose to ride one to work every day. It started as a way to both save the planet and to get exercise. However, it also became a way to stay present as every mile and every corner represented somewhat of a risk when riding the streets morning and evening.

We can admit that sometimes when traveling in an automobile, there have been times when we've driven back and forth from home to work or to a sports contest and realized that we couldn't remember the drive at all. We couldn't tell you which streets we turned on. . . what other cars were on the road. . . WE WERE ON AUTOPILOT in a car that was NOT self-driving!

What about the other thousands of decisions we make every day, starting with when to get up in the morning? Am I going to hit the snooze? Am I preparing and eating breakfast at home, taking it with me, or getting something to go?

How am I choosing to treat people at home, at school, at work, at the grocery?

Am I working out early or late? At home? At the gym? Or not at all? And the list goes on and on, doesn't it?

To what degree are we on AUTOPILOT . . . and to what degree are we consciously making choices with a clear mind and heart? And how are we planning for tomorrow or next year?

What is the value of planning today for all of our tomorrows? The value is in choosing for ourselves! By choosing which actions to take, we are delineating our priorities and driving our stake. When we show up and take action, we are living and growing into our destiny.

We believe that among the most important steps on a career journey is the step to create congruity between one's heart and mind.

1. Are you in a career where you say to yourself, I can't believe that I'm getting paid to do the work I love?
2. Do you sometimes think there must be something better out there?
3. Does your work mean more to you than just a paycheck?
4. Are you wholly satisfied with your calling and purpose?

We certainly kept these questions front and center in our life journey while seeking balance as spouses and honoring family priorities. Our culture can cause us to think that doing what we love and getting paid are mutually exclusive. We like to think having both is possible. Matching up paying our bills while engaging our heart and soul longings will help create a healthier, congruent sense of wellness that carries into our families.

Gratefully, we look back at our family legacies that nurtured us. These legacies were what helped us overcome our fears and embrace new opportunities. When we think about our entrepreneur ventures and multi-generational businesses, we can't help but lift up those who went before us. We grew up among families who were small business owners.

Both sides of Deborah's family were entrepreneurial. One owned a three-generation storefront enterprise, providing home plumbing repairs while selling washers, dryers, and refrigerators in serving a southwest Ohio community for multiple decades.

Deborah's grandfather on the other side of the family engaged in a summer painting business while also carrying out his part-time pastoral duties. Simultaneously, through all of this, he spent forty years as an industrial arts teacher in an urban community.

John's family built a thriving feed and milling business in northern Illinois that grew out of a simple farm operation in the 1950's. The focus of the business was serving local farmers' needs with regard to livestock feed as well as crop fertilizers.

John was the oldest of four siblings, and as a result, over the years, he spent a lot of hours working on the family farm. . . doing chores, baling hay, serving customers, shelling corn, truck driving, and an abundance of field work. He learned so much about teamwork and contributing to the greater good of the whole, both via the farming operation and the feed & milling business that his parents were steadily growing. His mother and father put food on the table and shelter over his head and helped him have extraordinary opportunities, including exchange student, choir tour, church camps & conferences, etc.

During those years, John did not receive an allowance nor a tangible paycheck on a week-to-week or month-to-month basis for his semi-regular farm work. While he did raise and sell hogs, which did expand his savings account, his opportunities to have money in his hands were extremely limited.

Later, his parents—and grandparents—who had prioritized higher education, helped him earn a college education in what turned out to be a huge financial gift towards his future. In effect, John's farm and business labors in his growing-up years were returned to him in the form of having his college tuition paid in full.

As John was coming out of his teen years and began to enter the *real world*, he had a lot to learn about handling money, as he really hadn't had much to manage on his own so far. During college summers and on campus, he worked so that he had some spending money in an account of his own. For him, it was a life-long journey of learning while earning. That likely accounts for the reasons he pursued and developed an investment management business during and beyond his years in education. Managing his own money—and now helping others manage their own—was a transition in John's learning to feel competent and capable in spite of his early journey in money management.

Over time, John was able to take his new skill set and apply it to his family and business. We are exceedingly grateful when we think of all the benefits we received from the various multi-generational family business models that preceded both of us. These family businesses showed compassion and appreciation for their employees. They made sure workers didn't feel taken for granted. They also modeled 'customer first' service. Through the years they were also dynamic to change as situations warranted with regard to their marketplace as well as to price points.

We could not have foreseen or tangibly planned each and every opportunity that came to us in our lifetimes. Like the generations before us, we too learned that we had to bring flexibility and take action in order to prosper. We focused on tenaciously pursuing what would help us keep our family secure and put food on the table. We kept as much control of our outcomes as possible without getting overwhelmed nor resorting to feeling like a ping pong ball being bounced around. In the meantime, we kept a constant conversation going with regard to where the next opportunity would lie.

As you've probably gathered in your reading of our book thus far, our kids were encouraged and invited to participate in our numerous family ventures. They were watching us lead by example in our marriage partnership. They were witnessing first hand both the challenges and benefits of entrepreneurship. And they were beginning to manage their own money and resources.

While we kept regular *jobs* through many of our working years, we were regularly on the lookout for additional income streams. Driving tractors, raising livestock, coaching sports, teaching behind the wheel, offering investments, and network marketing all factored into our options for income through the years. Paying attention to any door opening to us allowed us to stay grateful for the ways in which our family had all things provided.

We discovered while John was working and traveling for the college, that we could keep one parent at home while the other worked one job and still not have that interfere with family time. We were careful when we added side jobs to our resume that we could either include our family or that we could build in time to detach from work for our family to spend time together.

CHILD CENTERED

We were intentional in our early years as parents to put our kids first. This meant following our desire to see that one of us was home with them daily. While this might be more easily do-able in many situations, we complicated it by our willingness to look for heart-centered work no matter the complexity for our family. The first instance of honoring career discernment happened after John had spent five years as a public educator and simultaneously earned teacher tenure. At the same time, he felt a longing for further inspiration and foundation by choosing a seminary education. And we wanted to make sure that was feasible for the family to still keep a parent home with two young children. Deborah was willing to search for a teaching position. And she found a very desirable position as a fifth-grade teacher in a suburban Chicago school district where we lived.

We were able to achieve our goals as John cared for Angela and Andrew while attending seminary part time and Deborah taught in a local elementary school. John was a stay-at-home-dad somewhat ahead of his time in 1980. One year later, a college development post as director of church relations back at our alma mater was available, and we chose to pursue it. During that time, baby Aaron was in the womb and our family was blossoming to become a family of five. It didn't make us wealthy, but building the foundation of going after our desired jobs felt worth it.

In every Economics classroom the phrase, "there's no such thing as a free lunch," gets tossed around. In our young family, in the early '80s with only one *bread-winner*—a college employee on salary—we were earning limited income. So much so, as a family of five, we qualified for public school free or reduced-cost lunches. While we didn't access this program, it was something of a wake-up call with regard to our earning power at the time. We didn't travel much during those years or if we did it was done as inexpensively as possible.

We both came from families who valued every resource, so hand-me-downs were nothing new, just practiced more frequently during the days when money was tight. Our kids were still young, so what was struggling for us was normal for them. They couldn't really complain about not eating out or going on fancy vacations since they hadn't experienced that much. Making sure that family memories were made everyday became a greater priority for us.

Under these circumstances, we began to consider other career opportunities. We worked side jobs because we knew every penny counted which helped us live as frugally as possible. After three years in the college development position that involved John being on the road and out-of-town overnights, we were looking for a greater income-producing opportunity and more quality family time.

Unexpectedly, several community members asked Deborah to run for the local five-member town board in 1983. She got elected after having lived only a few short years in the community. During her tenure, she learned so much and helped solidify a small town's traditions and reputation via her position. Little did we know at the time what would come about as a result of Deborah's public service on the town board. She learned the ins and outs of what it takes to run a town as well as many of the businesses in town. This was a vital learning experience that opened our minds to possible opportunities that we had never thought of before.

During the town's expansion in economic development, one of the areas she became acquainted with was an agricultural opportunity. John had grown up on a farm, so while it seems a lot different than his work at a college, farming was actually in his blood.

So with the help of parents and friends, we secured financing and built a livestock operation from scratch. We became partners with others and entrepreneurs ourselves. With John's farm and animal husbandry background, he managed the livestock operation. We invested in the day-to-day barn management for four challenging years. In doing so, we came to understand the foundation of the business and took responsibility for every aspect of the venture.

Over the time we managed the operation, we enjoyed supporting the kids to be actively involved as contributors. They helped with livestock management, the feeding process, and sanitation steps. Each of the kids really rolled up their sleeves to participate joyfully and for a chance to make some pocket money to add to their personal budgets. This was the first time we had actually worked together on a job site towards a common goal, and it was so thrilling to make it happen.

The kids participated in our livestock venture where we learned to center on teamwork and cooperation. We practiced positive communication skills as getting each of us to the barn after school was an exercise in well-coordinated calendars and transportation. Angela, Andy, and Aaron learned responsibility, perseverance, and money management skills as they were paid for their work. We helped them budget their money. First, they donated to charity, then some went into savings, and the remainder was spent or saved as they chose. We felt this was an appropriate way to teach them about the impact of personal effort leading to financial rewards. It also helped to instill a sense of responsibility and satisfaction for a job well done. Little did they know that their previous work experience would lead to yet another *job opportunity*.

We learned so much as entrepreneur business managers and found ourselves in a better position to be financially more stable. We also found this to be a springboard to yet another vocation-changing adventure as we kept paying attention to our aspirations. Where we were at that time, we were open to possibilities and felt called to launch ourselves further along.

When it came to careers, we felt fluid, more like running water than a stagnant pond.

Following each other's career longings had become central to the ways in which we supported each other in our marriage partnership. After starting out as teachers, we headed to seminary, then to college work, and on into agriculture.

Deborah had entertained furthering her career for a while, considering counseling of some sort. Her longing came after five years of teaching, after four years of growth on the town board, and through her church activities, particularly in youth leadership.

Our day-to-day life experiences, coupled with our exposure to a holistic health center while in graduate school piqued our interest in the counseling field. The health center's practice of manifesting health and wellness into all areas of our lives really resonated with us. The fact that a full scope of wellness included physical, emotional and spiritual aspects of our lives was enlightening. We were drawn to more fully explore the field of counseling and personal wellness because of what we had learned.

As our livestock management venture was winding down, we began a search for opportunities that matched both our desire for new engagements and more sunshine than the Midwest offered. Previous family visits to Florida and California had given us that curiosity. When a dear friend suggested Arizona, we went for a visit. We found a return to public education there that captured our imagination. On our second visit, a generous job offer was extended, and we decided to make the move.

When we chose Arizona for new opportunities and to further our education, we knew we were opening ourselves up to numerous possibilities. We came to understand a little better what Henry Nouwen wrote: "You don't think your way into a new kind of living. You live your way into a new kind of thinking."

PARENT DIRECTED

When we arrived in Arizona, we were stepping into new jobs while helping the kids settle into a new school and new routines. We also arrived with energy to pursue professional and personal development. Shortly after getting our feet on the ground, we began our school counselor certification journey. We chose a growth mindset as educators willing to move forward to pursue certification with an understanding that it would expand our minds and talents.

Choosing counselor certification meant sacrifice. We had to be willing to give up evenings and weekends for classes. Our family had to adjust since our kids were without us during these times. Because the certification was a priority for us we were open to growth and saw life as a glass half full as opposed to half empty. The best way we have found to try new things is by staying open minded and keeping our focus on the vision at hand.

LAHMAN FAMILY SWIMMING

Within our first two years in Arizona, another family business manifested. Deborah's school-building principal remembered that Deborah had been a swim instructor and wanted her granddaughter to learn to swim. So in the first summer that we had a swimming pool in our backyard, Deborah started our Lahman Family Swimming business. Within a couple of years, she had not one, not two, but three personal swim assistants in the pool with her, helping more and more children of friends and colleagues learn to swim. Angela pursued swim certifications first, and then Andy and Aaron followed.

In total, through a period of fifteen summers, we estimate that Lahman Family Swimming taught nearly seven hundred children through those years. This included water safety for all, as well as water adjustment to the littlest ones and how to swim to those who were ready. Again, this venture helped put money into the kids' hands so they could practice giving, saving, and spending. As it turned out, between their savings and academic scholarships, they earned over half of the costs of their private college tuition and fees.

The lesson here is from the *you never know* collection.

You never know is somewhat like those days when a foreign object landed on your plate when you were a child. Your first question was *what is that?* Your initial statement might have been *I don't like it.* But if you didn't taste it, how could you possibly know if you liked it, right? You never know until you try it.

The art of allowing requires us to open our hands and minds. What is it that you allow into your life? You never know how something in your creative, enthusiastic, and tenacious hands could be something far bigger than you can possibly imagine.

In our family swim story, that is totally the case. From a chance recollection by the principal, a business was born. A business that paid dividends in so many ways. . . for those children who benefitted from the learn-to-swim lessons. . . to the young instructors who earned college tuition monies and lifetime worker skills. You certainly never know how an opportunity in front of you may create a lifetime of wellness, purpose, and abundance.

That doesn't mean that it was always easy. Angela, Andy and Aaron often wished that they could be out playing with friends or watching television on a lazy summer school vacation morning. However, there were people who had signed up and paid for swimming lessons and there was work to be done. Oftentimes, when we think of side jobs, we only think of the money they bring and not the time and work that they entail as well. . . or the lessons learned and experience gained! Our youngest, Aaron, reminded us that oftentimes he felt anxious and stressed when parents watched him teach their children how to swim. Over time, that helped him build confidence, but we would be remiss if we didn't mention that there were still challenges and tough times while building our Lahman Family Swim School.

The following is a reflection from Angela's *Facebook* post about those days as swimming instructors:

> "April 2020:
>
> Let me tell you a story. In 1990, my mom started teaching a colleague's granddaughter how to swim in our backyard pool! By the next

summer, all three of us kids were in the water with her and multiple other kids (some of you remember firsthand the Lahman Family Swimming Business)!

Friends, our entrepreneurial ambitions were created, not born. We started then to set the stage of what was to come in Living Well Now: people over profits, intentional living, wellness focused, half-full consciousness, community driven and always grateful to God for our blessings.

When I look back on those days, I remember arguing with my mom that all I wanted was a *real job*, one that required me to show up for a shift and wear a uniform I was cold in the afternoon when the sun went down because I was soaked to the bone (parents were sweating on the side in 110+ heat while I shivered) and kids wouldn't recognize me in the store because I was wearing more than a swimsuit and hat! I complained as any teenager may have, unaware of the life skills being planted inside me of financial stewardship and savvy business competence.

Who knew that almost thirty years later, I'd be using those insights gained to lead a growing team of people, passionate about freedom and

committed to their own dreams . . . still working alongside my family! Here's to expansion
and those who choose to show up for their vision every day!"

In addition to work and alternative income streams such
as Lahman Family Swimming provided, we were also on the
lookout for investment opportunities. Our accountant gave
us suggestions as to the tax advantages and potential income
streams of rental properties. A short while later, we were able
to purchase a single-family home in a city nearby. And we did
it as a family with each member contributing a percentage of
our down payment. Angela, Andy and Aaron participated as
young adults with an opportunity to see how moving into an
ownership position changes outcomes. This meant learning
how to do work on the rental property before renting it out.
This meant learning more about budgeting, assets and liabili-
ties. This represented another family short-term income stream
and the prospect for a long-term legacy. We did a fair amount
of cost-effective upgrades as a family, and then welcomed our
first renter.

The name we chose for our business was Mustard Seed
Ventures. The mustard seed is one of the world's smallest seeds,
yet it grows into one of the largest plants on earth, with limbs
strong enough to provide shelter and be of use to those that
needed shade. This is how we saw ourselves, wanting to grow so
that we could help those in need. The idea that nothing is impossible has motivated us through the years. When you present

yourself open to the universe and carry a *can-do* attitude in your heart, there's no telling what abundance of opportunities may come your way.

COMMUNITY SUPPORTED

Swimming. Biking. Walking. Running. Through the years, we have done our best to practice great health.

It's been said that *True Wealth is Great Health.* We believe that. There was one period, during the 1981–1982 school year, with three children under the age of five at home and John on the road part time in college development work, Deborah's immune system became compromised. Her physical health was depleted. She went from one medical source to another who recommended various solutions to no avail. Her best remedy turned out to be natural supplements—our first introduction to homeopathic healing alternatives. And we also experienced our first exposure to a network marketing company. We briefly dabbled with the business opportunity, ultimately becoming avid product users. From that day forward, we have been students of many prevention and intervention strategies that have become significant aspects of our day-to-day health and wellness journeys.

Looking back at the challenging early days with young children when we lived on a tight budget, amid our natural mindedness, we began conversations to help prosper our lifestyle, to seek entrepreneurial opportunities, and generate greater financial stability.

We definitely saw the glass half full when it came to our naturally-minded lifestyle and we were exceedingly willing to pursue the opportunity to be involved in sharing it with others.

LIVING WELL NOW

We had continued making health and wellness our priority through the years. In 2006, a wellness company brought us back to the network marketing world—twenty-five years after our first encounter—where this time, we found greater opportunity and promise than we had experienced before.

In 2006, while Deborah was seeking alternative support for her endocrine system, a friend suggested a prevention and intervention option. From that day forward, as we learned more about numerous other wellness products, we began to share with family and friends the awesome health benefits available to them.

Introducing natural hormone solutions was but the first step in a varied journey into the wonderful world of natural products for optimum living and wellness. By becoming the CEO of our health, we were able to promote our own longevity while promoting healthy options to family and friends.

Simultaneous to our wellness company discovery, a life mentor mentioned that she was retiring from her career and that she was taking time to determine how she was going to redirect her energies. That struck a chord with us. We were also considering retirement — from public education — and choosing how to redirect our energies. What better way to move forward in life than to champion our own health and wealth intentions while bringing those same opportunities to friends and family around us?

We committed fully in terms of time and energy to our wellness business(es) through concerted efforts. As a family we attended wellness conferences and read numerous books on every related subject.

As so commonly occurs, when you are open to all possibilities while entertaining Divine appointments, surprises abound. In 2008, our family created Living Well Now in our desire to share healthy lifestyle choices and wellness products with the world. The Living Well Now mission centers on the belief that all persons are created to live in optimal health. We are passionate about exploring the synergistic connection of mind, body, and spirit. As a Living Well Now team, we offer, promote, and encourage transformation in the areas of wellness, purpose, and abundance.

Combining our health/wealth passion, business owner knowledge, and counseling strategies, we are incredibly blessed to teach, empower, and equip those who are seeking to fulfill their dreams of becoming financially independent. We represent a synergy of skills that help us coach others in the journey of life, while seeking to empower every person to celebrate their gifts in creating a legacy of prosperity.

As entrepreneurs focused on designing our future, we have combined the things we love most—family, education, stewardship, and wellness— to create successful businesses. We enjoy organizing and leading events and sharing our business opportunities and successes with family, friends, and folks in not just the United States, but around the world. No matter who we're talking to, in all of our Living Well Now endeavors, we are grateful that we don't ever feel like we are sales focused. We don't sell. We listen. We help people find solutions. We encourage. We teach.

As we have built a network with other members and families who are also seeking health and wealth opportunities, our Living Well Now team has grown exponentially. We are deeply grateful that our community is envisioning abundant possibilities as they seek increasing financial independence.

LAHMAN FINANCIAL SERVICES

John began to build his own financial independence when he got an invitation to step up his financial IQ while he was a high school educator. He was invited by Teachers Helping Teachers (THT) to offer supplemental retirement investments on his school campus. Being one who had not spent much time managing his own money growing up, let alone had any experience in the financial arena, this piqued his interest. He wanted to learn. So, he said yes. Little by little, through informal training with THT, he began sharing investment products with colleagues with whom he worked.

After a few years of growth, he was invited to provide mutual funds to teachers and staff. And, again, he said yes, and his business grew.

After Andy had worked in the corporate world and taught school for a number of years, he became interested and sought the opportunity to come alongside his dad as an office assistant and representative of Lahman Financial Services. And then, several years ago, John's mentor, the architect of THT, asked John if he wanted to buy his business. And, of course, John said yes!

Now, while serving hundreds of teachers and other individuals, his income stream has become a significant portion of our family resources through more than two decades . . . all because we said yes, years ago, remained patient, and stayed faithful to the little things. Being an entrepreneur encompasses just such practices and habits. The same was true with our rental home that we had purchased as a family.

MUSTARD SEED VENTURES

Little did we know after saying yes to our Mustard Seed Ventures property ownership, the adventure wasn't done. We kept renters in the home while managing the day-to-day needs of the house and the renters themselves. And just over a decade of rental property ownership later, and after a number of renters had enjoyed our Mustard Seed Ventures' rental home, we sold the property and exercised a 1031 exchange to use our profits to help us purchase our retreat/rental destination in Carlsbad, California. When we look back on our first property management venture, we recognize the significant work and effort we invested, and we celebrate the abundance it helped us accumulate.

We feel passionate and blessed to be using this new property as a retreat destination. Both Living Well Now and our non-profit Living Well Now Foundation (LWN) are prospering by offering retreat and workshop renewal opportunities for LWN members and friends. The foundation is dedicated to both offering and supporting human wellness and educational experiences that expand horizons and cultivate global awareness.

A further intention for the foundation is to scholarship youth and adults so they can participate in mind-expanding travel and educational adventures. We know there are remarkable opportunities that the foundation can provide in offering these adventures for others. Our belief is that individuals who have courage enough to access learning experiences and who are also committed to growth can potentially realize an untold boost in personal development and/or business success. This manifested our first retreat camp.

HEALTH, BALANCE, LEADERSHIP CAMP

There was a time when simultaneously, each member of our family was an educator. We were in classrooms ranging from junior high/high school language arts to high school math and communications to elementary gifted to high school special education to high school yearbook to elementary and high school counseling and administration, and we made a difference. Each of us saw the needs of children from many different vantage points. And we knew there were ways in which we could serve further. As a K-12 educator family, we thoroughly enjoyed guiding children and teens. That interest set us on a new journey to serve in a broader way.

With Aaron's college experience in non-profit enterprises, initiating a summer camp for active high school teens became his focus. And we all jumped in as a family to support the endeavor. We worked with high school administrators for approval and then went about recruiting young people to participate. In particular, we offered camps intended for high school students who weren't learning leadership strategies and social emotional wellness. We could offer workshops on creating a balanced lifestyle while undertaking leadership opportunities. And for two summers in a row, we sponsored Health, Balance, Leadership Summer Camps in the cool pines of Prescott, Arizona.

Our purpose was to help young people refine their leadership skills while broadly encouraging successful life habits to help navigate their futures. Our staff was committed to modeling healthy and balanced lifestyles while promoting transformative leadership, incorporating integrity with concern for one another.

One student's comments provide some insight into the togetherness that flowed out of those camps:

"Camp was overall a great, eye-opening experience. I really loved how I got an inside look on other people's perspectives on life and being able to become one big family."

There is power in kindness and wellness in helping kids launch like geese to find support and encouragement as they step into the real world.

TOOLS

So, let's be clear. We didn't do this alone. It's not about the useless adage of *pulling yourself up by your bootstraps*. Of course, you have to get to work. However, it takes connecting with people, joining a club or a small group, meeting people and launching yourself, and getting beyond any fear that might hold you back.

Find your tribe: Who are the five people you spend the most time with? They will influence you the most! Choose wisely.

Eat better and concentrate on your health. Find a coach and/or a therapist. Create lasting relationships that inspire you. Seek to learn. Read for inspiration and information.

So, whether working alone or working synergistically with others, ask yourself: What opportunities await? What might we discover if we were to really dig into our souls and then stretch towards new outcomes?

Dream Big: One of those soul moments could lead us to Dream Big. Choosing to pursue big opportunities can be scary. Therefore we must find the courage to step towards our goals! If we don't first believe it, we will never see it. Those action steps towards new opportunities speak to the soul of our entrepreneurial spirit!

Chasing after our dreams while staying centered is critically important. Imagining, while planning, helps put wheels under the wagon; helps promote accomplishments. Once we imagine and plan and get used to that lifestyle, we then are able to become. wake up one day and we are not trying to do anything . . . we are. It's all about taking action toward goals while staying balanced in living.

Dreaming big helped us . . .

1.   Create our Living Well Now network marketing business.
2.   Purchase a retreat destination near the beach.
3.   Create the LWN Foundation non-profit.

Synergy: One of the reasons we like Stephen Covey is because he speaks and writes about growth possibilities. You will find references to his works throughout this book. In particular, his book *The 7 Habits of Highly Effective People* suggests that 1 + 1 = 3. You may think that that is just bad math; however, that is the power of synergy. In educational circles, we used to help facilitate cooperative learning. The power of synergy is in the ways two creative teammates can create a shared outcome to represent far more than either of them could accomplish alone.

Covey points out that synergy explains why we are able to produce something none of us could produce before or even adding to what each can produce separately. He also stresses that strength lies in differences as long as there is a common vision and principle-centered value system. If we can rally around a goal and/or a purpose, the outcome will be something to look forward to.

Focusing on your new goals and opportunities can make something that feels remotely possible in the future... a reality in the present!

Living life by design, not by default, pays dividends. Choosing to take a risk, face our fear, or just get serious about something we want can create a huge shift in outcomes.

What's your Big Dream? Don't hesitate. Go for it. Pick yourself back up when you stumble. Try again. You've got this!

REFLECTION QUESTIONS

1. How has your business impacted your family? For good?
    In struggle?

_____

_____

_____

_____

2. What do you need to change about your business/work to
    better accommodate your family?

_____

_____

_____

_____

3. In what ways can you involve your children in your work?

_____

_____

_____

_____

4. Do you see any other business opportunities that could incorporate your entire family?

_____

_____

_____

_____

5. What sort of business leadership style are
    you role-modeling?

    _____

    _____

    _____

    _____

6. Again. . . what is your Big Dream?

    _____

    _____

    _____

    _____

CHAPTER 5

RESILIENCE

"Discover the depth needed to cultivate and strengthen our self awareness while persevering in navigating our emotions."

In seeking to reflect on human resilience, we know it is every human's experience beginning on the day of their birth. And we recognize it as everyone's lifetime experience from that day forward, not that we are particularly aware of our resilience minute to minute.

When we begin our lives as infants, we are wholly dependent for all sustenance and care. We need other humans to provide for us. And then, ever so slowly, we grow increasingly independent through the years and we begin to practice personal resilience. We live a lot of our earliest days relying on and learning from our caregivers: parent(s), siblings, grandparents, aunts, uncles, cousins, friends, et.al. We subconsciously take note of their choices and are ultimately guided by their decisions, energies and behaviors. We begin to practice resilience, modeling what they have shown us. It's a complex undertaking.

Since our most critical learning years and brain development occur from birth to age six, caregiver influences impact us the most — those who guide and care for us on a daily basis. When we're an infant or toddler, whomever provides primary care early on will be the one(s) from whom we learn the most and from whom we take lessons. As that toddler grows they learn from others around them.

Our youngest grandchild, Bennett, has exhibited great tenacity in her short lifetime. No doubt, being the youngest contributes to that as she strives to keep up with an older brother and older cousins. In addition to her *keeping up* efforts, she has also expressed the phrase, "I've got this" more often than anyone we've ever been around. Her family reminds us that Bennett first used the expression "I've got this" before her fourth birthday. When the training wheels on her mini bicycle were accidentally bent when one of the family cars backed over them in the driveway, they had to be removed to allow the bike to stand up straight. A family video still survives of three-year-old Bennett pedaling that little bike her fastest while repeating, "I've got this" over and over. Now, that's learning positive self-talk at a very young age.

COMMUNITY SUPPORTED

By the time we become parents, hopefully we have put all of our resilience muscles to work. In some respects, nurturing children and raising a family is a little like making *resilience* stew. We don't exactly need a strict recipe to follow, but at the same time, we do need to pay attention to the ingredients and seasonings because we want the stew to turn out well. In a similar way, on our life journey, how we handle adversity will affect our kids' outcomes and teach lifetime lessons to them.

Day by day and year by year, we grow to make our own choices and decisions. We don't live life without facing challenges and overcoming them, and that continues until the day of our death. As we view this journey from a parenting perspective, we come to find and understand resilience challenges. Because not only are we in charge of caring for ourselves, but now we're tasked with empowering our children to be resilient and to handle their own adversity. Taking care of others while paying attention to our own needs is quite a balancing act.

That being said, have you ever noticed that your kids sometimes can function in complete confidence and autonomy until they suddenly need you? And quite commonly, it seems that happens at a point where you're the most engaged in an important phone call or in a very focused moment or processing through your own emotions? This is more than just uncanny. They sense events. They *feel* your circumstance and challenges. Your vibe may be giving off a sense of dread to them. They're close by to be assured that everything is going to be OK. Understandably, they want to be comforted. They don't necessarily care about your well-being ; however, they do crave their own safety and security. You are the critical piece in their world. They depend on you in so many ways.

Children don't pay much attention to a parent's self-care. Sure, there may be an occasional breakfast in bed on Mother's Day or Father's Day or a shoulder massage after they know we've had a hard workout. Yet when we are the most needy can be the time when the kids need us most. You want to say: *Actually, right now, I've had it up to here, and there's no room for you at this moment!* And so we frequently walk that fine line between our needs and theirs.

We know that daily needs of our children are more than just the basic food, shelter, clothing triad that keeps children alive. It is also the active molding of character, personality, talents, spiritual, emotional and physical well-being of the child that encourages the child to thrive. Paying attention to all of this gives us hope that our kids will graduate into the real world and make good choices going forward. Providing the right foundation is key to eventually watching our kids find their purpose and succeed on their journey.

As adults, we know that we learn the most and become much like those five people who we spend the most time with. Remember our recipe and the effects of our seasoning? As we choose to shape our lives, seeking those who are parenting-aware will bring the greatest hope to us. Those who share a bigger vision for raising the next generation and who exhibit positive, forward-thinking mindsets will pay back big dividends over time for our family.

Making good things happen as a parent, as we have expressed earlier, depends on taking a proactive attitude toward our parenting role. If we're always reacting to situations, then it's probably time to step back and get creative to re-check our approach to the circumstances and our attitude in order to move into a parenting prevention mode. We can't stress enough the importance of anticipating what's ahead and preparing our kids to the greatest degree possible.

PARENT DIRECTED

As we led parent education workshops throughout the years, we sought to be exceedingly encouraging and positive about each parent's efforts to be a family. We wanted them to understand the responsibility they needed to take and the opportunity they had to effect positive change in their family. Those who attended our seminars knew how much we recognized what their participation in prevention strategies could mean. We were heavily committed to appreciating attendees for showing up and doing their best each and every day.

We became focused on helping prevent problems before they cropped up. We sought to reinforce positive parenting practices and offer prevention strategies as well. We encouraged participating parents to pat themselves on the back for recognizing the great job they were doing as parents already and for showing up to learn more through the parent education activities that we offered.

Did we have any idea what adventures awaited us as parents ourselves? No, we did not. And, it can be said, no one does. As marriage partners and parents, early on in our relationship, we focused on gathering tools for our journey. Early in our marriage, when we were attending a Marriage Enrichment experience, one of our extended family members asked if our relationship was *on the rocks*. We pointed out, quite the contrary, that we were trying to gather as much information as possible to strengthen our relationship. We began personal development before we even knew what it was. This is why we were proactive. We knew we would need more information regardless of whether any problem was evident. We chose prevention. Why wait for the problem to manifest?

CONFIDENCE

We will focus on the ways in which we claimed confidence for ourselves and instilled it in our children: Angela, Andy, and Aaron. We were tenacious about giving our kids safe spaces to share feelings and opinions. And we sought to teach them to not be afraid of conflict and to give them tools to manage conflict themselves. All three of them took college conflict resolution/mediation classes to provide intervention in a dispute in order to resolve it. It was not strict arbitration. Rather it necessitated bringing the conflicting parties together, allowing each party to talk while the other listened, and then seeking a compromised understanding of what the conflict was about and how to resolve it going forward. Over the years, they have each utilized the mediation process and/or taught mediation directly. Through the incorporation of these conflict resolution skills, resilience was built into so much of what we shared with our kids on the journey.

When we think about managing ourselves and practicing resilience, what we choose to stay away from are feelings and perceptions like the following:

> Parent: As long as you live under this roof, you'll do as I say!
>
> Parent: No daughter (or son) of mine is going out in public looking like that!
>
> Parent: Don't talk to me like that!
>
> Teen: You always say no!
>
> Teen: I don't care what you think of my friends, you can't choose my friends for me!
>
> Teen: You are the most old-school parents anyone has ever had!

Have you ever heard expressions like these? Do they resonate with you? Have hurtful expressions been more the exception than the rule in your life story?

So what happens when feelings get all messy and friends or family get involved and maybe get dumped on? Where do we go from here? How do we make things better? How do we apologize? How do we patch things back up? When we feel we've been wronged, it can be very difficult to make things right. If kids have grown up with limited information for how to get past their feelings to resolve a problem, they can get stuck in never-ending cycles of personal disorder. Finding the right recipe for healing and wholeness can be difficult.

RESOLUTION IN ACTION

One illustration of conflict happened vividly on John's high school varsity soccer team one season. A new player on the team who was a significant contributor had violated team rules, and upon missing the bus —his final violation —had to be dismissed from the team and a championship holiday tournament match. He was angry and said some things that hurt others. John made a decision that he needed to be cut from the team.

Over the course of a couple of days the following week, hard conversations took place among team captains and team members with the athlete and with John about allowing the player back on the team. When we can soften our hearts, we sometimes see the bigger picture and recognize where authority matters and where understanding an individual comes into play.

In this case, by engaging in communication with all parties, reaching an understanding of hearts and minds, and the delivery of a heart-felt apology to the team by the dismissed player, misunderstandings were resolved and the full team was restored. It took resilience by all parties.

In our own family, there were a few examples of misbehavior and consequences that followed. For example, in elementary school, during recess, Aaron was caught throwing stones. He did it in tandem with a new *friend* he had made. He learned that choosing friends is important territory. The teacher who witnessed the behavior could not get Aaron to admit his wrongdoing. He lied and denied the infraction, rather than confessing.

In the process of resolution of this matter, he learned that telling the truth is the right thing to do. He wrote a letter that he read to the teacher, apologizing for his actions, and he began to learn at a rather young age that his character and integrity would be judged by his honesty and by his behaviors.

Bringing someone to an apology and fostering understanding can communicate peace into a situation or into a family. As parents, we discover there aren't always happy endings. Sometimes hard truths need to be learned during the growing-up years. In our family we understood that. Sometimes lessons are learned when we hurt and also when we cry.

TEARS CAN BE GOOD

OK, we've all been there as parents. Our child trips and falls and skins their knee or they don't get the exact ice cream flavor they wanted. They are suddenly into a full-blown meltdown in their trauma/fear/hurt/anger/etc.! Our first response? Well, there are lots of different ways to go with this one.

On most occasions, we chose to let them cry. Yes, we just held them, adjusted our surroundings as necessary, and allowed them to *feel the feelings*. Yes, that might mean leaving the premises for a safe, less occupied space. We recall heading for the grocery exit even though we were leaving a partially full grocery cart inside, necessitating a return trip at another time. But when a child is not in a space to be told no, we're on a budget and we're not getting that box of cereal, then we have to take more definitive action. If we immediately try to take over the situation by telling them

not to cry, then we've forgotten something . . . their immediate mindset.

In sudden upset, we chose to first deal with their initial fear
because maybe nothing exactly like this had happened to them
before. They were used to being *whole* and now they weren't.
They're confused. Words may or may not be helpful. Certainly,
alarming them about how bad it is is not the best response.
Launching into words of blame like 'why weren't you watching
where you were going?' are definitely not helpful. At the moment, they are mostly caught up in the crisis at hand. Figuring
out why it happened is for another time.

Saying, *Ooh, that must have really hurt when you fell?*

Or just holding space by not saying anything at all can also
be soothing. Getting the details later and asking what happened may be appropriate at a later point in time. After the
initial response has diminished, the door will open for conversation about the incident. In most cases, it is better to allow the
feelings first and save the conversation for later.

CHILD CENTERED

In Dr. Michael Popkin's *Active Parenting* blueprint, the defini-
tion of an *Askable Parent* is: "To be the kind of parent whom
children will seek out for support and consultation when they
have a problem. A parent they will want to ask questions of."

As parents, we seek to provide the support so that our kids
know we can be trusted and we're truly there for them!

QUALITY TIME

For us, seeking to be askable parents meant making time to have ongoing communication for clarity. We sought to make it clear to our kids that we *had their backs* and that we wanted to walk with them through thick and thin. We supported their growing independence, which gave opportunity for significant dialogue in both their joy, like making varsity sports teams, and challenges like dealing with conflicts or teen drama. Our goal was to help them establish confidence in themselves and trust in our relationship with one another.

One of the ways we did this best was to involve our kids in shared experiences. They ran a 5K with us at the ages of five, seven, and nine. They participated in our fledgling businesses. They visited our extended families with us. They helped us lead workshops. We took road trips and vacationed together. They joined Deborah, teaching swimming lessons. These shared experiences provided us with quality time together which created common ground and greater opportunities to tune in to one another and have conversation about our joys and challenges.

HOLDING SPACE

As is so often the case, significant events are well remembered. While we often focus on a child's misbehavior, we continue to remind the reader that the parent's actions speak loudly here. Do we label our child? Hopefully not. Do we find fault with everything they do? No, we look for their best behaviors and acknowledge them.

We confirm that behavior matters, so what about our behavior as parents? How does it teach a child just as much if not more than our words?

The following is a story about a parent's resolve to support a child's development. A dear friend of ours had a very capable older daughter with giftedness in many areas including science and math. When advanced chemistry came along in high school, the challenge was immense. While the daughter became frustrated and furious with the homework learning, mom was there in many ways.

Mom would hold space like she'd never had to hold space before. After all, parenting through elementary math problems and high school chemistry are completely different journeys, right? Mom listened to daughter reflect on the complexity. Mom had a college education but she didn't major in biochemistry. Daughter vented and vented. Daughter tore up her homework and threw it away. Mom recovered the homework and taped it back together to allow resuming the work. Mom refused to give up on her daughter, and ultimately, the daughter refused to give up on herself.

We know firsthand that the mother's support continued through medical school as the daughter was invited to call any time for support. Sometimes, a call was made to allay fears about an exam or just to allow processing time to vent, relax, and rest when sleep seemed not to come.

To this day, in one of the greatest parenting triumphs we have witnessed, the daughter became a practicing family doctor as well as the mother of three thriving young adults. There's no way to properly measure the incredible support and inspiration provided by the mother who showed so much resolve and patience in guiding her daughter to such remarkable academic and relational successes.

Just think where she would be if her mom hadn't been there to recover her high school homework? There's really no way to know what that outcome might look like. What's apparent is how much it meant to the daughter's life because of how her mother handled it. This certainly is a full manifestation of what an askable parent looks like.

ANGER

Expressing our feelings is exceedingly complicated. Oftentimes, we reflect what we saw as children in our homes. How did we witness angry feelings expressed when we were growing up? And what have we learned from the angry expressions we experienced? How do we handle them in our own lives? Do we just let it all hang out and unload it on anyone nearby? Are we passively inclined to let angry words 'in one ear and out the other? When we're young, figuring out how to express angry feelings in an acceptable manner will serve us for a lifetime.

In our own family, anger was on the table. We talked about it. For instance, Aaron struggled with a teammate who regularly bullied him. Aaron needed to figure out how to deflect the abuse and stay focused. It wasn't easy. Sometimes, he just needed to vent about it. Sometimes he needed to hit a pillow. Being acutely aware and actively engaged as parents and teens opened doors to communication so that we could support

Aaron through his adversity. Although challenging, Aaron had to manage his anger to keep from allowing the conflict to escalate into a physical altercation, which could jeopardize his place on the team.

In developing resilience, anger is one of the most challenging emotions to manage. Where to begin?

1. It is a loaded term.
2. It is a misused expression of emotion.
3. It has the power to change one's life positively or negatively.
4. There's usually something underlying the anger if we look deeper.

It's well documented that underneath anger is hurt and fear. In other words, if someone is manifesting anger, if they dig deep enough, they can usually connect their anger to a fear or a hurt somewhere in their past. And sometimes, it's way back in their childhood years that they first encountered that fear or felt that hurt. If left unresolved, it can manifest many years later. Sometimes we don't choose to visit either one, and so we hide behind our anger.

It isn't that we've been taught how to feel or don't know how to feel . . . it's that we have a feeling and it makes us upset, which turns into anger. If we turn that anger onto people instead of being honest about those feelings, we hurt others. Individuals and families do this in different ways.

MANAGING

Usually, what anger needs is an outlet. It is OK to be angry. What is important is how we choose to manage the angry feelings. Rather than control it, some folks just spew it or scream it. Others choose to stuff it and ignore it. When we stuff it, it has the potential to build up on us. If pushed down, it doesn't necessarily go away . . . it's just lying in wait. If we try to sweep it under the rug, everyone knows that the dirt will still show to others. Eventually, the anger rears its ugly head.

Trying out alternate strategies is important to the anger management journey. Giving ourselves permission to take a break can be soothing. What outlet do you give yourself? Journaling? Working out? Reading? Running? Meditation? The one you choose to use is less important than just having a *go-to* whenever you feel your body reacting to the anger emotion. When we stay *in* the complexity of feelings, we have trouble de-escalating the matter. By stepping away, we remove ourselves from what is triggering our intense feelings and can perhaps even identify what fear or hurt is underneath this intense, angry energy.

In recognizing anger in all of its forms, we know staying centered on the individual expressing it is critical to processing and resolving. All family members may be inclined to occasional bursts of anger and moments of frustration that trip them up and stir their emotions.

The Anger Tree, an idea of Jean Zimmerman and adapted here by Education for Conflict Resolution conveys that sometimes we use anger to cover up other feelings. It is often easier to express these hidden feelings through anger. We need to listen to the real feelings, understand them and express them. The tree shows the anger in the branches, but its roots are the real feelings which are difficult to see and express.

The Anger Tree

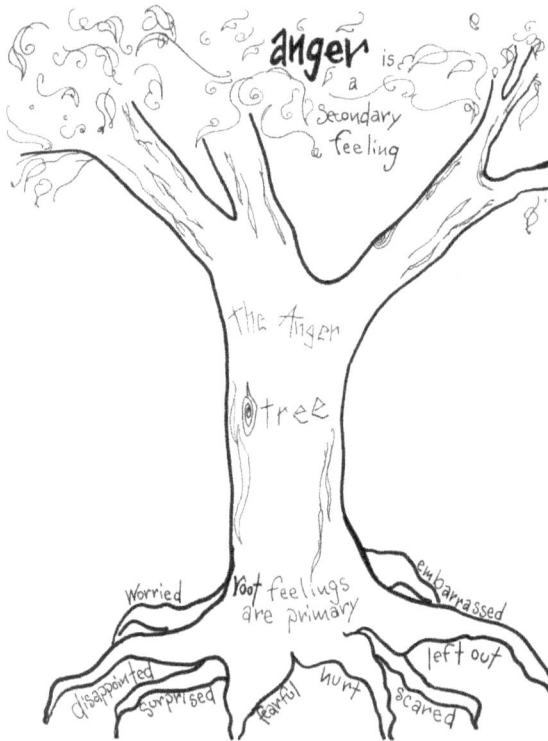

Jean Zimmerman

Education for Conflict Resolution

The root feelings that are primary are included in the list below. Each one is real and genuine. Giving attention to the primary feelings permits a parent or caregiver to help an individual alleviate or minimize the anger that can manifest thereafter.

1. Worried
2. Disappointed
3. Surprised
4. Fearful

5. Hurt
6. Scared
7. Left out
8. Embarrassed

As parents, may we seek to not hold our own feelings inside nor torment with overt angry outbursts. Rather, may we develop our own coping strategies. We can courageously channel our own feelings as a way to transform and change not only our lives but also those we are called to guide.

DON'T FEED IT

As grandparents, we have enjoyed teaching and sharing a crazy, funny little children's book entitled *Don't Feed the Monster on Tuesdays*, written by Adolph Moser and creatively illustrated by David Melton. It has been one of our grandkids' favorite books. A *monster* in the story is the one that wants us to feel bad about ourselves. And as the book progresses, the monster enlarges as various feelings start stacking on top of one another with examples like:

- *My head is too big.*
- *I don't make good enough grades.*

- *I'm too clumsy.*
- *My parents scold me.*
- *If we listen to these voices, the monster's voice becomes louder and louder!*

The monster gets bigger and bigger as we feed it our fears and insecurities. The monster likes to take great big bites out of our self-esteem. What we learn is that if we stop feeding the monster—even if it's just on Tuesdays to begin with—he diminishes in size and intensity. Our self-esteem can be restored little by little. Before long, we have replaced the negative feelings we have about ourselves with positive feelings. After all, when you say nice things to yourself, you start feeling better about yourself. Up goes your self-esteem and, of course, down goes the monster.

Is it really that simple? In many cases, it can be. We need to understand that discarding an old image and re-imaging ourselves can take time. If we were first nurtured having our self-esteem beat up, then re-recording those messages in our mind can require a longer healing process. When we focus on patting ourselves on our backs when we do things well, or communicate well, or finish our chores, etc., we build our self-esteem and find resilience in doing so.

TEENS

While teens may seem to always be seeking independence, they are also looking for support, encouragement, and acceptance from their parents. Those teens who have heard negative, cold prickly messages through their childhood years may have already begun to write off their parents for any insights they might want to offer. However, if a base of love, support, and communication have prevailed in the parent/child relationship prior to adolescence, then the stage is set for a continuing desire on the part of the adolescent to seek information from parents and to feel the love intended.

As parents of teens, it is important to do more than just stand alongside and watch as they ride the proverbial roller coaster of adolescence. Processing with teens while we are on the roller coaster together helps to better understand what they are feeling and experiencing. Being present in their lives and carefully listening for understanding lets the teen know they're not alone. Being an engaged parent in this situation is different than just being a spectator. We understand we have only so much control of the teen roller coaster. However, we can choose how we take initiative to better understand their journey, thus offering support.

FEELINGS

As we have seen with anger already, feelings can be complex. How we label *feelings* can have a long-lasting impact. When children are irrational, we sometimes call it a tantrum or meltdown. When a child is in a highly charged situation, there's usually a trigger that causes the overreaction. In most cases, children don't recognize the tipping point. That's why labeling the behavior isn't fair since it seldom involves a choice. Rather, it is expressed when in reactive mode, not in a rational state.

Someone who is illogical or not reasonable is considered to be irrational. In that moment of irrationality, bad choices get made, and these situations can end up poorly. When a child exhibits such explosive behavior, we might jump to conclusions.

We recognize that children are sometimes labeled negatively for tantrum-like behavior. We understand that it is less about the child and more about the intense expression of feelings in the moment. When that happens, whether with family or friends or acquaintances, it sometimes does have repercussions.

Angela had one of those kinds of days that we all remember as children, when we didn't want the day to ever end. We were at a picnic with lots of room to run around, make new friends, and celebrate being out of doors on a very beautiful day.

Late in the afternoon, when we were ready to leave, Angela didn't want to. She was running away from us and trying to hold her ground in a show of independence. In her irrational moments, tears flowed and her anger was clearly expressed amid her disappointment. We finally got her to the car, and of course, as commonly happens at the end of a big day and after letting her feelings out, she eventually fell asleep on our drive home.

As parents, when we looked back on the situation, we had to ask ourselves a few questions:

1. How well did we communicate with her to join us for our departure? Did we give her any heads up, like a *five-minute warning* that we were getting ready to go?

2.   How hungry or thirsty might she have become playing so vigorously for so long?

3.   How did we allow or facilitate her saying goodbye to playmates? And were there other ways we could have handled the situation in bringing closure to this event?

It seems there are often questions like these to be answered when children's behaviors are outside of the norm to which we are all accustomed. Before we label the behavior as a tantrum, meltdown, etc., we need to self-examine our role to better understand the stimuli involved in the behavior.

Understanding the need for expressions of feelings is important. Being aware of what we can do to lessen the impetus for such behavior is equally important. Allowing the child to vent and be sad or angry is the right choice in the long term. And in the short term, expressing understanding and giving the child permission to feel his or her feelings can be very healthy. Equally important is looking carefully at what we can do the next time we are in a similar situation to give our child tools to support their growing maturity.

In Angela's first semester of college, we journeyed to Indiana to visit her. Andy and Aaron, both in high school, remained at home. They were not pleased that we had left them behind. Both of them would have appreciated being included in the trip, especially since it was back to old friends and their old stomping grounds.

When we returned home, they were most gracious, however, they were still disappointed that they had not been able to join us. Sensing their frustration and spending some time discussing their feelings with them, we wrote the following letter to them that same evening:

> *Dear Andy & Aaron –*
>
> *Thanks so much for welcoming us home so nicely today. We know from our conversations prior to, and during, our weekend in Indiana that you would have loved to be with us. We made a decision that you would not go this time. We know that you sense that you missed a good time with extended family who you love – and who love you. You did miss a good time. Thanks for sharing us with Ang!*
>
> *There will come a time in your lives when you will be making hard decisions like this one. In fact, the decisions you are making right now aren't unlike this kind of a decision that we made this time. You both face choices in and out of school that require you to sometimes choose between friends and their behaviors. You both are doing an awesome job of thinking clearly in such matters!*
>
> *We want to encourage you to continue to vent your feelings and let us know what you want and need. We will work with you to try to meet those needs. Of course, we need you to help us be aware*

of them. If you continue to need listening about the weekend just past, let us know.

We love you!!!

Dad & Mom

This letter was our way of acknowledging their frustration and opening the door to further conversation going forward and incorporated in our "I messages".

TOOLS

I messages: This served to help each member of our family take ownership of their feelings and in some cases, to name their desires or expectations.

Mom, Deborah, remembers expecting kids' rooms to be picked up and cleaned up on Saturdays. As the kids understood it, that meant rooms needed to be in order by midnight Saturday night. Momma needed a little more clarity than that. Her *I message* went something like this:

"I feel disappointed and upset when you don't get your room picked up in a timely manner on Saturday. What I need is for you to have it cleaned up by Saturday at noon."

The combination of I feel . . . when you . . . I need . . . helped to be more specific with regard to almost any family matter that could arise.

For example, when school or work commitments caused a delay, any of the kids might have said: "Dad, I feel disappointed when you picked me up from practice much later than you said you would. What I need is for you to show up within ten minutes after practice is over so that I'm not always the last team member waiting at the school for my ride."

The purpose is to help de-escalate the situation. It helps us go beyond the feelings and use clear communication strategies to work it out.

Proactive Steps: We encourage our kids to express their feelings, usually with a listener present. In anger, sometimes we supported them to hit a pillow—rather than one another! It was not a time to hurt others or to damage property! Sometimes taking a walk and getting some fresh air was helpful . . . or journaling, playing a sport or game, etc. Any kind of a time-out to get some space was helpful.

We strongly encourage everyone to bear in mind that angry feelings, properly channeled, can be a huge motivational source utilized for positive outcomes. Many significant accomplishments were motivated by anger. Taking proactive steps out of anger can carry us to incredible outcomes.

The challenge of making change in the face of difficulties is overwhelming. If we take our circumstances and channel our frustration into positive steps, we have the formula for potential success.

Be honest: The phrase, *just because it's your emergency doesn't make it my emergency* communicates an *I* message in a different way. It could also be said: "When you come to me with your emergency, I feel hooked by your drama. What I need is for you to plan a little more carefully ahead of time and/ or to come to me with a solution for your situation."

Own it: On the self-development journey, taking responsibility and saying I goofed are among the greater practices to develop. In our human experiences, owning our behaviors is the first step. Sometimes we want to blame others for what's not right or what's not working. Sometimes we just want to deflect responsibility when things aren't going well in our family or when we, frankly, just mess up. When we don't prepare and things go awry, blame starts flying around. While we may not feel like anything was our fault, it seems the blame lies on our shoulders because we overreacted, spoke too soon, etc.

Plastic Containers as a Tool: When Aaron got into junior high school, he would sometimes have difficulty quieting his mind and settling to sleep at bedtime. Sometimes, he needed to process further and talk it through. We developed a means for setting issues aside in order to quiet the heart, mind, and spirit. This included talking about any worries and then putting them away into a plastic container which got *burped* as a representation of these topics being protected and kept safe and put to rest under his bed for the night. This technique proved effective as Aaron will tell you how calming that process usually was for him.

CLOSING

We spent a lot of time discussing emotions in this chapter because processing emotions will speak to how resilient we will become. We don't choose to label a child for feeling emotions. Rather, we choose to provide tools for managing the emotions. Likewise, whether expressing hurts or crying tears, giving space and acknowledgement will offer the most support for long-term health and wholeness. While we can't impose resilience, we can model it and hope our kids will catch the messages sent their way to utilize it in their adult journeys.

We know that there's a challenge in paying attention to our own lives while guiding the lives of our children. We must be responsible for allowing our children to live their own lives while monitoring our own. If we consciously or unconsciously try to live our lives through our kids' lives, we will find ourselves hopelessly trapped. Whatever we have or have not achieved is not for our kids to pursue. Our kids are growing up as unique individuals in a different generation. It is better for us to seek for them all that they can become than to pressure them to do as we did or to seek what we did not accomplish.

We close this chapter centered on the need for resilience in all aspects of parenting. In spite of our best efforts or planning, things happen. Some days Murphy's Law is at work when it seems nothing is going right. Through the parenting years, when we hit the pillow at night, we were grateful in our prayers for being carried through each day while asking for guidance to make tomorrow just a little bit better. We also learned that when it comes to parenting, staying light hearted and silly can be helpful and lead to healing as well.

REFLECTION QUESTIONS

1. What does resilience mean to you and your family?

_____

_____

_____

_____

2. How are feelings dealt with in your household?

_____

_____

_____

_____

3. How does your family manage anger? Is there another emotion that sits under your anger tree such as fear or hurt?

_____

_____

_____

_____

4. How does your family view stress and how do they deal with it?

_____

_____

_____

_____

5.   How are we honoring the unique person hood of our kids?

_____

_____

_____

_____

CHAPTER 6
THE VILLAGE

"We celebrate the power of interconnected, diverse communities that positively impact families."

We see in nature numerous examples among species, whether bees, beavers, birds, et.al., how to work together to grow, share food, build homes, and exhibit cooperation. So how do we apply these lessons from the animal kingdom into our families, or more deeply, into our communities and villages?

Here's one example we'd like to share with you. We have been deeply enamored with the following story of geese in migration. These facts have been attributed to numerous individuals including a pastor, a biologist, a Buddhist monk, and an environmentalist.

Geese Teamwork Fact 1: As each goose flaps its wings it creates an uplift for the birds that follow. By flying in a "V" formation, the whole flock adds 71 percent greater flying range than if each bird flew alone.

Lesson: People who share a common direction and sense of community can get where they are going quicker and easier because they are traveling on the thrust of one another.

Geese Teamwork Fact 2: When a goose falls out of formation, it suddenly feels the drag and resistance of flying alone. It quickly moves back into formation to take advantage of the lifting power of the bird immediately in front of it.

Lesson: If we have as much sense as a goose, we stay in formation with those headed where we want to go. We are willing to accept their help and give our help to others.

Geese Teamwork Fact 3: When the lead goose tires, it rotates back into formation and another goose flies to the point position.

Lesson: It pays to take turns doing the hard tasks and sharing leadership. As with geese, people are interdependent on each other's skills, capabilities, and unique arrangements of gifts, talents and resources.

Geese understand on a distinct level how to 'work together' and how to take turns. What's not to like about having uplifting partners who are going in the same direction and also welcome sharing leadership responsibilities? This is a great example of a healthy village seeking greater outcomes.

In our marriage partnership, we have been taking turns leading or honking from behind, like the geese. Working together creates greater outcomes. For many years we have marveled at the power of sharing common goals, staying in formation, and taking turns as we share leadership. What we have seen is that there is power created when individuals with different talents have the same goal.

In the ways that geese exhibit strength by working together, we believe the same is true when humans together seek and manifest their most creative and unified efforts. That only happens when we spend less time noticing how we are different and instead focus on the positives that each one brings to the table that strengthens our families and our communities. We can maximize outcomes by doing the hard work of unifying rather than focusing on our differences. Multi-generational experiences (grandparents/grandchildren) have a synergistic power all their own as young and old learn from each other. We must choose to seek to see and discover the goodness in one another.

Our children benefit when surrounded by more than just parents and immediate guardians. They are influenced by society, by educators, by religious leaders, by extended family and friends. It's important to pay attention to those you choose to have around you that impact you and your family in a positive way, those that help you and your kids fly like the geese from our example.

To a great degree, we choose who those influencers are. It's why most parents interview pre-schools these days. They're examining the village their child will join. We are so grateful for those who have been the influencers in our kids' lives, whether extended family, teachers, faith partners, friends, colleagues, or neighbors.

COMMUNITY SUPPORTED

As we look back over our life journey, we recognize how much we took from our faith upbringing. The multi-generational communities that we shared a faith with provided a deep, supportive framework via members and friends who provided light and encouragement in our earliest years. *Community* came to mean so much to both of us, and so everywhere we went, we tried to share neighborly love, care, and concern for one another into our school and work environments. As we raised our own family and moved about, we chose to engage with local communities that nurtured our children and us.

When we look back on our kids' pre school experiences, it is hard to imagine more loving and intentional teachers who helped provide such a fine foundation for our youngsters. From modeling caring and sharing behaviors to just taking genuine interest in each child's well-being, we could not have asked for more diligent and supportive leadership. This carried over from preschool to the elementary and junior high years. We saw the impact the village had on our children. For example, male elementary teachers that set great examples for Andy and Aaron. Coaches who were focused on the experience for the kids, not just on winning or losing. Musical teachers and directors who sought the best in both performance and behavior. Those teachers, coaches, directors, and administrators offered educational opportunities of all kinds that provided short-term excellence and a foundation for lifelong learning.

We were blessed in the Midwest and Arizona school communities we encountered and engaged. We considered our work environments as opportunities to express community on a daily basis. As educators, we saw colleagues —and the students we served— as partners with us on a journey towards wholeness. We were seeking to create more compassion, wellness, and peace. We took into our day-to-day worlds the attitude that we could make a difference. We felt we could contribute to positive outcomes. This manifested in various ways, including the parenting workshops we offered.

Among the workshops we facilitated were subsets of the family unit that we sometimes forget about. It is easy to think of our religious communities, our schools, and our workplaces as forms of the village that support and guide us. At the same time, the parent-child dyad needs support because they can easily be neglected. When we were asked to do parenting classes, we chose to incorporate our children into our presentations. This helped to build a stronger community among all parents and children, including what eventually led to the following Moms and Daughters experience.

MOMS AND DAUGHTERS

With the advent of social media in recent years, some women are increasingly in *keep- up* mode. Keeping up with other women means being the best parent, spouse, and the most engaged, screen-savvy savant. Unfortunately, living up to those expectations is just exceedingly unrealistic. We are frustrated by the unhealthy place that many young women—and oftentimes their teen daughters—find themselves in. Life can be highly competitive and easy to compare yourself to others. This can lead to resentment, depression and even meanness.

This is unacceptable, and our daughter Angela and mom, Deborah, wanted to work to change that. A class was put together to bring mothers and daughters from various backgrounds to discuss what ways we can foster healthier relationships with one another. This idea proved to be more revolutionary than we first thought. Imagine groups of women banding together to help raise powerful young women, who could in turn do the same? This would literally change the world!

There is power in the generations in the mother/daughter relationship. The interconnection of that relationship is one of constant growth and change. Some women find that connecting with each other is a challenge, especially in the teen years. When it comes to the village, how important is the mother/daughter connection for empowering one another through the highs and the lows?

We believe it is vital to gain more insight into one another's needs and wants. Our outcomes included dialogue and openness, focusing on communication skills —like active listening—along with conflict resolution and relationship building.

In a *village* format, we structured the workshops so that after a brief introduction to the class and one another, moms and daughters were split up with Deborah leading moms' discussion and Angie leading daughters' conversations. We made sure that participants felt listened to in our conversations. Numerous questions helped to stimulate our discussions. For example:

Teens:

What is going well for me and my mother is…

The area of greatest difficulty in our relation-ship is…

One thing my mother just doesn't understand is…

I know the one thing my mother wants for me is…

Moms:

What I like about how I was parented by my mother when I was a teen…

What I would change about how I was parented by my mother when I was a teen…

Where I need support in parenting my teen daughter is…

An activity my daughter and I like to do together is…

Both:

If I could take my daughter/mother out to her favorite restaurant, it would be…

The ultimate goal was to make sure that at the end of the workshop, they could look each other in the eye and say, "I hear you" and/or "I see you." Even if it only meant they found out each other's favorite hobby or restaurant, the hope was that they would continue the conversation and take it further in the future. It was rewarding to find out how much daughters and moms did know about each other. When they can make connections, share time and safely vent with one another, mothers have the opportunity to articulate her family values and thus strengthen their daughter's values. What are some insights that you want your daughter to know that you haven't communicated?

Workshop reflections are always helpful. One of the mothers wrote the following after one of the workshops:

> *"Just a quick note to thank you both for the class last night. I thought we had some good discussion and sharing. When we were getting in the car to go home, my daughter said, 'Wow, Mom! You and I have a GREAT relationship! That was nice to hear for a couple of reasons—one, I can tuck it away to remember in those not-so-great moments, and two, it's nice that she is noticing that our relationship is much better than many others.*
>
> *It was interesting to learn other's viewpoints on mothering. I think it's so important to be able to have that support! I have been in mothering groups for many years, and I've found that while support is intense in the early years, it's easy to lose those connections as children get older.*
>
> *Angela, my daughter really enjoyed talking with you as the daughter in the equation – comparing moms and finding a lot of similarities.*

Thanks again for your time and your enthusiasm."

WHO IS THERE FOR YOU?

As parents, if we're supporting our kids in positive ways, who's there for us? There seems to be this embedded competition between parents these days. We look at Mom or Dad posts or blogs, and they make us compare ourselves, our families and our villages to someone else. More often than not, it leaves us wanting . . . we feel like we are missing something. We believe that parents are missing something. Most of us are missing the same thing: a parent village, which is a community of hope and support!

We believe that the power of the village is intended for parents too. We can only pump ourselves up so much from the inside. Having outside voices there for us can more than double the strength we need to handle the challenges and opportunities that come along. The parent village really matters for the support it provides. By attending parent education classes, we are equipped with tools for our parenting toolbox. And we receive encouragement from facilitators and other parents to celebrate the little victories and to feel equipped for the day-to-day challenges. And each parent feels comforted that they are not alone on the journey. As facilitators, we saw the power of bonding and mutual support that parent education provides.

When we combine your support for me with my support for you, we get a multiplication effect. With an accountability partner, we create a much larger impact than going it alone.

This collaboration creates a ripple effect that can impact all of the geese with whom we are flying! When a few of us parents gather together and treat our families with positive support, our care for our children cannot help but be changed for the better. Our kids see the role modeling that happens, they see the healthy interactions, and they have consistent messages from all of the adults as their community expands. These are all reasons that we as adults need a village that we can lean on and rely on for support.

PARENT DIRECTED

Our intention for all people of the world is that they would find a fellowship of individuals who offer warmth, hope, love, and encouragement like we experienced. When you are surrounded by people who care about you and your family—those with whom you can engage while developing safe places to risk while growing in trust with one another—nothing else compares.

We all expect to send our kids out into the world or into the *village* so that they can be successful. As parents, we really have the opportunity to guide our kids into the *real world*. It's up to us to help them work on personal skills like assertiveness, kindness and collaboration so that they can interact well with others. We can also encourage them to dive into village experiences and to take action themselves to learn from direct interactions. And among all of these skills and experiences, if we are both teaching and modeling the behaviors we seek for our kids, we will begin to see them take flight to find their own independence and embrace the village for themselves.

WHAT YOU ATTRACT

When we look back, we realize that pouring village goodness upon the kids helped them to become more kindhearted, and they attracted friends who shared many of their same values. Their friends subscribed to collective kindness and thus to larger community/village rules. There were disagreements in the village, and those differences were either resolved or relationships changed. When becoming a healthy village is the goal, we choose to work through misunderstandings to keep them from being blown out of proportion, particularly when miscommunication occurs.

We did keep an open door to conversations about village difficulties that came along. We decided to be active listeners so that we could have conversations about any bumps in the road. We know kids will experience the best and worst of The Village at times, and they will come home with questions. The more askable we become, the more likely we can help them sort out the realities and see their choices in the matter.

We know it is common for kids to come home and complain about teachers or acts of bullying they have experienced. We allowed venting in order to be an open door for sharing and to help our family move forward by putting the incident in their rearview mirror.

It makes for a good village when we prepare our kids and families to interact in healthy ways with their peers. Initially, it is up to us to provide consistent healthy adult-child relationships so that they have a good model to follow. This is what grows those children into healthy young people who can, in turn, create a village of their own to interact in the same manner. In a village where love abides, there are healthy outcomes.

We have been guided by many wise family and friends, beginning with our own parents and grandparents. They showed us love and respect while manifesting *community* in so many forms. We took lessons from them and believe each of us are uniquely gifted and talented and called to make the world a little bit brighter every day as we commit to passionate living in community.

Kids watch and learn so much with their eyes and all of their senses as they notice all of our actions. At the same time, what we say may not carry as much significance. Showing the way rather than telling the way helps us better get to our desired destination. For example, how we interact with our village/community/neighborhood sends a clear message to our children. Are we friendly, welcoming, and hospitable? Do we compliment and encourage, or do we gossip and criticize?

How we get along demonstrates to our kids how to get along. They will act and behave in a similar fashion.

Showing the way instead of telling the way becomes ever more important when our children get older. It especially rings true when they begin to become interested and attracted to their classmates. There is a lot to navigate during puberty, and dating makes it trickier.

NO, YOU HANG UP!

Is there a way to define *healthy dating* for our kids? As parents, with our own dating experiences, how do we go about helping our teens venture into the land of relationships? What is it we want for our kids? We could all probably agree that what we want is for our kids to be engaged in healthy, positive relationships.

We supported our kids to celebrate friendships first. Aaron will tell you that we strongly discouraged him from getting into an eighth-grade exclusive relationship when we resisted allowing him to be *going out* with a classmate. We strongly encouraged him to create a wide variety of friendships with numerous individuals, both male and female. We didn't want him to feel limited to one person at the age of fourteen. It was our position that we wanted Aaron to have friends at that stage of his life, not limited exclusivity with a girlfriend. We know that many times this opinion is not shared by all, and we respect that.

As parents, we choose and ultimately celebrate the village of friends with whom we are connected. We want the same for our kids. In the process of our parent education leadership, we found ourselves immersed in the topic of dating because of our own kids. In several settings—a couple of times in a national youth conference venue—we were privileged to lead several hundred young people and advisors in dialogue about dating.

When we asked questions of participants, we got some ordinary answers and a few surprises.

For example:

What are some positive aspects about dating?

1. Have fun/hang out
2. Get to know someone and their family
3. Look for/think about positive qualities in a future partner

My ideal date companion would have these characteristics:

4. Easy to talk to and sense of humor
5. Honest & trustworthy
6. Caring & respectful

Our children had friends from varying backgrounds, so finding things in common to do as a group could at times be difficult. Our kids found many healthy options for their peers to spend time together.

I'm bored!: Ever heard a teenager say *there's nothing to do*? In high school, Andy developed a list of fun things for his group of friends to do together. What he figured out was that if he took some leadership and did some inviting, others were quick to join in and participate. He generated some sizable get-to-gethers of friends hanging out. A few of his things-to-do were:

- Table games & popcorn
- Scavenger hunt
- Frisbee golf/Ultimate
- Bake cookies
- Do community service
- Roller skating/ice skating
- Dance
- Swimming
- Hiking
- Karaoke

DIGITAL VILLAGE

Today we find a whole new challenge when it comes to the communities in which we find ourselves. There was a time when *the village* meant the neighborhood we grew up in. However, now, this can represent an entire world because of our connections online and the ease with which we can navigate the community through social media.

That doesn't mean that the digital village is any less dangerous nor is it healthier. We need the same type of training for our kids to interact inside that community as the ones we have in person.

In the screen-focused culture we have become, human connections are changing. We don't have the same day-to-day interactions that used to be so customary. Just saying good morning to one another or asking about each others' families has slid further off the slope of norms. Some of the digital villages we encounter are not genuine. However, the creators do all they can to make them seem legitimate. Paying attention to our kids' online interactions, as parents, becomes increasingly important.

One thing that hasn't lessened is the sense of *drama* that seems to be ever present. When we see such behavior on screen, it becomes more the norm. A junior high public school teacher noted how less reading and more movies has meant less maturation of thinking skills. When we read, we *picture* the story. When we literally *watch* it, there is no need for the imagination to be as active. What kids catch is not the use of their imagination but rather mimicking what they see on the screen. This can cause a lot of unhealthy actions and adverse behaviors in the village.

Have you noticed that folks are still doing small group or online book studies but very few movie studies? Book groups give us village experiences. These screen experiences don't as much. They change our interactions. They change how the village functions. The impact of *screen living* means we are more alone and less connected to the village. Our interactions are changed one way or another. How do we show common courtesy or how do we know what appropriate interpersonal exchanges even look like?

If we view society through the village lens, we know that our television shows, our computer video channels, even our social media are all teaching things to us and our families.

So what story are we getting from them?

As you can see, communication has changed immensely over the past couple of generations as we have become more screen focused and less interpersonal. Since there is no escaping our interpersonal lives as family units, how do we maintain positive connections with others? The answer is, it depends. There are a lot of variables and some that we typically don't consider. The following addresses those not-so-obvious variables that influence our communication.

NONVERBALS

We grew up in families who reminded us: "If you don't have anything nice to say, then don't say anything at all!" When kindness is not on the tip of your tongue, then better to not say it. When we feel like criticizing, it is better to see if there's another approach to the situation. Seeking to integrate compassion into our exchanges returns double fold and generates more positivity all around.

What are the best steps we can take to bring about healthy and productive communication? The normal perception of teen communication is that it's either very, very limited in content, unintelligible, or an expression like *you wouldn't understand.* While that doesn't reflect the best of family communication, it can be a bit difficult to engage in good quality dialogue on an everyday basis. What we know about communication is significant here in seeking understanding within a family or within a village.

When analysis of active communication the following data has been documented. Words used in most communication only comprise 7 percent of the actual understanding reached. Actually, tone of voice is much more important than the words, coming in at 38 percent. Body language registers a whopping 55 percent of the total communication that takes place. Our efforts to reach understanding must take into account numerous factors, none of them to be taken for granted.

For a family —or for a village—to understand one another, careful attention must be given to delivery of the words as well as in listening with all senses for understanding.

CHILD CENTERED

Andy, on the occasion of his 16th birthday, decided that he wanted to initiate a wholesome endeavor to enlarge his friendships and provide recreation for all. He had Aaron's full support and encouragement. Andy pleaded and gently persisted that we build a sand volleyball court in our backyard. The boys were *all in,* so they spent days with their dad, clearing the area, hauling sand, and running to the hardware store for lighting and poles. Neighbors jumped in to help as the village created a friendly volleyball venue to rival those of Malibu while located in Glendale, Arizona!

We wanted our house to be a healthy meeting place for the village kids since we were educators and we knew how important it was that there were safe places students could go around town which took the place of the not-so-safe ones. The sand volleyball court in our backyard helped offer village opportunities for those teens who chose to be part of Andy's and Aaron's closely-held community. All varieties of games on various weekend afternoons and evenings provided space for the village to interact. This intentional village-building was received well by so many.

Since our home was one of those safe places, it meant that when other kids were over, we treated them like our own children in a lot of ways. For those friends who were closest to our family it meant closer interactions. Remember the timer we talked about earlier in the book? Well those friends had an opportunity to *share time* around our dinner table when they were over. You participated in telling us how you were doing or what you had accomplished that day or what plans you had for the future. Even if you just called in and we were around the table, you still might get to take a turn.

Various stimulating and insightful conversations took place and even just plain, ordinary stories were shared. Ideas—no matter how contrary or just plain weird—were welcome. And all knew it was a safe place to put thoughts on the table. Trust was huge here. It allowed for great sharing. Unfortunately, trust may be in shorter supply today. And we, the village, are the only ones who can restore it in small increments.

As in any village or community, there are a lot of opportunities for conflicts to happen. The majority of the time, it has more to do with miscommunication. One of the tools we can teach our kids is the power of healthy boundaries which we believe this digital age has made more difficult.

A boundary is similar to a property line…this tells you what area you can play in and have fun where it is healthy and safe. We have to show people where their property line is in our lives. That way, they know what they can and what they cannot cross.

When our kids spend time with other kids outside of our homes, they are influenced and affected. Behaviors rub off when they spend time with other kids from the village. In being fully transparent, we need to understand that the 'village' needs boundaries. Boundaries are important both to maintain positive behaviors and good outcomes.

When conflict happens and relationships struggle, be it among teens or adults, then:

- Fighting can happen
- Gossip is more prevalent
- Disagreement festers

It is tricky. For example, how can we honor one another when disagreements surface? Can we agree to disagree? In current culture, as we write this, lots of polarization is apparent. It seems society asks us to sit on one side of the fence or the other. Finding a way to listen to one another in love creates the opportunity to find commonality and community.

We've talked about a few ways to bridge conflict in our Brokenness and Resilience chapters, but we want to remind you of those ideas:

When in conflict:

- Stop and listen (use the timer if you need to)
- Seek to understand, not to dominate
- Talk about those issues with safe, wise people
- Don't make decisions in the heat of the moment; pause and think

HEALTHY BAD GUY

Sometimes conflicts come in the form of child and parent. Our kids want something, and we know that it is not good for them or it won't serve them in the long run. We step in but not because we are annoyed, or frustrated, or taking out our own emotions on someone but rather because we know that they need healthy boundaries and guidelines.

The big step to take on the journey of loving through our differences is to become a healthy bad guy —being willing to take a firm stand when it has implications for our children's health and well-being. Parents occupy dual roles. Sometimes they're the heroes their kids look up to, other times they're the bad guys who have to say "no."

Choosing to be the one who is setting family goals, delineating boundaries, yet encouraging independence while promoting negotiation is extremely complex.

Seeking harmony amid all of the moving parts is critical… and rarely is it easy.

We did not succeed every time; however, we were persistent enough to get our message across enough times to create the atmosphere for understanding. As young athletes, Andy and Aaron were never in knock-down, drag-out warfare. However, they did have to have cooling off periods and step away from the game (basketball, soccer, volleyball, etc.) at times to just breathe.

We remember walking into the kitchen where they had a mini basketball hoop hung up and five seconds on the microwave timer to hit the game winner, and there was usually a disagreement about whether the basket counted or not. They began to understand that taking time out had a way of giving them some perspective and a return to calmer waters. We accepted that perfect balance was impossible to achieve. Rather, reasonable harmony was the more day-to-day attainable goal.

TOOLS

Golden Rule: We centered on *treating others as we would want to be treated,* the Golden Rule. In family situations, that wasn't always easy to manifest. At the same time, by practicing active listening strategies, we helped provide a framework and expectation for our family to grow into such practices. Secondly, by incorporating positive communication concepts, we became more attuned to our kids' needs and sensitive to their circumstances. When our awareness of others can be practiced and reinforced over time, the outcomes can be life-changing. And the children can be better prepared to make choices when they experience life outside their home.

Good Wolf/Bad Wolf: Have you heard the suggestion that we have a good wolf and a bad wolf inside of us, and the one we feed dominates? In preparing the kids for their adult villages, we sought to help feed them all of the good we could deliver. We wanted them to learn early in their lives the importance of feeding their good wolf of light and hope, not their bad wolf. We chose to encourage them to seek to be surrounded by positivity. It helped that the communities we plugged into also reinforced similar expectations whether in school or outside of school activities. We knew that our children would be interacting with others and wanted to make sure that they had like-minded healthy peers, especially when they were young so that we could minimize the drama and issues that they would face.

Collaboration: The rudiments of clear communication is at work when all parties participate in a family conversation. By strengthening our communication and our bonds within our family, our children can go out into the village and handle complexities and stay strong. Giving voice to family matters and resolving creatively is a healthy approach to making a family function well.

We learned that the best practice is seeking consensus whether that meant all being on the same page or at least attempting to get everyone on the same page. Consensus implies that both parties are in agreement with the solution. If we only compromise, then what we may find is that one party or both may have given up their position and ended up with less than what they desired. Collaboration to generate a group consensus is the better end result where we seek an outcome better for all.

Engaging any kind of communication for clarity requires careful and sensitive listening. And not just hearing, but listening for understanding as well. Bringing empathy into the listening equation is likewise important.

An empathic ear notes how the words, voice tone and body give clues to the individual's state of mind. To give feedback accurately assures the understanding and reflects a sincere connection. If we say we're *OK* but we really aren't, then we are delivering a mixed message. If we're *not OK*, then it's on us to say so. Sometimes our listener(s) can help us identify our true feelings by providing supportive feedback of what they are emphatically hearing . . . not just by repeating the words we are saying.

What we desire in the way of love and communication in our families does not always happen. Communication in love with our family takes a great deal of time and effort. Communication in love is generated by parents' focus, flexibility, and intentionality. Sharing praise rather than criticism is helpful. Acknowledging love by appropriate physical touch and words of encouragement is also positive feedback. It helps when those collaborative times are when the entire family is together.

Family meetings: Meetings as a family can net positive results to keep good flow among all parties. Such meet-ups can be a productive way to ensure internal family communication is working well. At the same time, they require intentionality in planning. They can be used to share a joy or a concern. Concerns need to be brought as an item of interest and must be included in a timely manner for a meeting agenda, not just a spontaneous beef with a sibling. A family that engages in an open-minded process cemented by good communication can be helpful in rectifying a problem, and even better if the behavior can be discussed early in the conflict to interrupt the behavior. Better also to see the issue as an opportunity to reach understanding.

Join social gatherings: A number of years ago, we created LWN Foundation, focusing on the priority of providing significant personal development opportunities through small group retreats, travel seminars, and educational endeavors. We seek to offer an environment for others to learn abundantly, claim their leadership gifts, and celebrate their commonality amid all of our diversity. Our goal is to see that other villagers have opportunities to be strengthened. A greater intention is that this would continue for generations and generations, in perpetuity. Because we choose for others to take life to the next level and keep their dreams alive.

CLOSING

The ultimate parenting goal is to deliver a competent, engaged, and evolving teen with growing communication skills and socially acceptable behaviors.

By working to develop positive communication patterns as parent and child, the stage is set at adolescence for a healthy, engaging relationship that encourages growth, freedom, and responsibility. Reasonable independence and the opportunity for decision-making contributes to the teen's ability to thrive.

Our granddaughter Elena, a current high school senior, has had an incredible educational journey. Pre-school staff and primary grade teachers all encouraged and inspired her learning, both in and out of the classroom. While excelling in her academics through junior high and high school, she chose multiple opportunities for leadership. She has embodied that leadership and speaks with power in her voice and confidence in her strides.

When she was twelve years old, she shared her desire to visit Nepal with a group committed to studying climate change and human trafficking issues. Elena asked Grandpa John to go with her. John and Elena were able to go nearly five years later because she was dedicated to her desire and wouldn't let it go. They traveled into the foothills of the Himalayan Mountains for a learning journey of a lifetime. Elena's unwavering dedication to everything she becomes passionate about is unlike any other student her age. She is teaching her Village every day that they can do what others simply dream about.

When geese fly in formation, they create their own unique form of teamwork. As each bird flaps its wings, it creates uplift for the bird immediately following. When the lead goose gets tired, it moves back into the formation to save its energy and benefit from others' uplift. What are the ways we can apply these principles to our lives?

These geese traits are learned and evolved through many years. We humans have learned how to get along through the years in ways that give hope to future generations. Our brains and hearts can work together to optimize our behaviors. Sometimes we stumble. We might get into fight or flight mode via our natural instincts when we pay more attention to ourselves than we do to others.

When we look for ways we can exhibit the teamwork needed to make life better for everyone, we begin to exhibit our best life. When we acknowledge each person's value to the community and celebrate their gifts, we are practicing these geese facts in order to make everyone's life just a little bit better.

Here are a few more for your consideration:

Geese Teamwork Fact 4: The geese flying in formation honk to encourage those up front to keep up their speed.

Lesson: We need to make sure our honking is encouraging. In groups where there is encouragement, the production is much greater. The power of encouragement is the quality of honking we seek.

Geese Teamwork Fact 5: When a goose gets sick, wounded or shot down, two geese drop out of formation and follow it to help and protect it. They stay with it until it dies or is able to fly again. Then, they launch out with another formation or catch up with the flock.

Lesson: If we have as much sense as geese, we will stand by each other in difficult times as well as when we are strong.

Think of the power generated by having everyone behind you, encouraging you and urging you on. Who doesn't want to feel praised?

And think of the love and empathy offered while you are ill, injured, or just *down in the dumps* to have tangible support to see you through your challenges.

We see that happening in our communities on a daily basis. When adversity visits a family, oftentimes the Village rallies around them. Fundraisers happen, meals are offered, and friends come alongside to lighten the load and offer assistance in someone else's hour of need!

On some occasions, we get the impression from various sources that there's a lot of hate in the world. What we see both in chance encounters with strangers and in our day-to-day lives is that there's actually a lot of love in the world. We see so many instances of caring for one another. We rise above worst-case scenarios and make them best-case scenarios. We share light instead of darkness. We become a lighthouse for others to keep them from danger or guide them to the harbor.

When we each are honking our support, sharing in leadership, staying purposeful in our migrations (daily coming and going), sending light and love to others, we can surely build a better world one moment at a time. We hope and trust you can appreciate why we think the *Geese Story* holds so much value for anyone who understands the Village for all that it represents with regard to loving one another and offering community in such substantive ways.

REFLECTION QUESTIONS

1. What sorts of support systems do you have in your life?

_____

_____

_____

_____

2. How are you helping your children with healthy social interactions?

_____

_____

_____

_____

3. Are you addressing social issues like healthy dating, struggling friendships or stress coping skills at home?

_____

_____

_____

_____

4. What types of teamwork are you building with other parents and families in your social circles?

_____

_____

_____

_____

5. How can you make your home a safe place for your children and their friends to spend time together?

_____

_____

_____

_____

CONCLUSION

"Your children will become who you are;
so be who you want them to be."

--Anonymous

Hello Again Our Cherished Readers,

Now that you've completed this book, how do you use the information you've encountered in these pages? Do you rush right out and start doing everything the Lahman way? We hope not. Do you introduce your family to all of the concepts you read about? No, of course not. At the same time, we do encourage you to assess your life and take from these concepts what fits you and your situation. Use what pertains to your circumstances. Modify and accommodate these elements by adjusting to the complexities of your family unit.

The Dalai Lama suggests that if we change one thing every week, in a year's time, we'll be a new person. In relationships, we know progress can be challenging. There are significant changes we can make in our parenting that will give us renewed hope or a recharged relationship with our children. This will require patience, perseverance and persistence.

Imagine applying for a job with this description:

1. Being on call 24/7
2. Providing adequate food, shelter, and security for others for at least 18 years
3. Emptying all pockets before shorts and pants go in the washer

This abbreviated list can be overwhelming. As 24/7 suggests, it can also seem never ending.

As a parent, it's not about doing everything. It's about doing something! Be willing to try new things! In the process of our entrepreneurial/parenting journey, we were trying new things. We were able to find solutions that might not have been apparent to others. And we did encounter those who weren't exactly supportive of taking new approaches. For example, when Deborah served on the town board, she had another board member who had been on the board for a while. When suggestions were made to offer solutions, he often was quick to say that *we already tried that and it didn't work.*

When we chose to take new directions in parental problem solving, we did not worry about whether it worked before. We were most interested in seeing if we could make it work now. We took action and did our personal best. That was all we could give.

Our hope is that by having written this book, we have provided you with encouragement to do your best. We also hope that the information provided helps to set you on a new path if that is your choice. And we encourage you to feel stimulated towards personal growth choices. If in addition, this book helps lead you to discussions with other parents to share the journey, that would be extra heart warming.

We close our book with our strongest admonition to encourage you to do three things:

1.   Pat yourself on the back. Appreciate who you are in this world, seeking every day how to be a better person, spouse, child, grandparent, friend, colleague, parent, leader, etc. We all need to stop and celebrate ourselves more often. If you haven't been noticing the things you're doing well as a parent, it's time to do so. The fact that you picked up this book as a resource is another good reason to be proud of yourself. If we can't honor ourselves first, how can we move on to honor others, including our children, our family or the village around us?

2.   Forgive yourself for the times when things didn't go quite like you wanted —when you didn't get the outcome you were intending. By practicing resilience you can continue to move closer to peace, harmony, and appreciation. Finding the inner strength to weather the storms and emerge whole and healed becomes the greater sought-after outcome. We believe that working through the pain is where life happens and where growth can show up.

3.   Implement the wisdom that you have encountered in this book —what resonates with who you are and how your family operates. Monitor and adjust as needed to make it fit your situation and relevant for your circumstances. We grew our family together through a business and entrepreneur mindset. We knew that following our dreams would take work, so we made work something that we could do together whether it was teaching, farming or building our wellness company.

The village we surrounded ourselves with was ever growing and more important with each passing year. We tried to make sure that our children and family were supported by a diverse and caring extended family. When we commit to learning all we can and to intentional outcomes, we get more fully engaged in our own legacies. That may incorporate how a family behaves, works together, and engages their primary community.

We get but one opportunity to guide a child. Many have offered strategies. We leave you with the words of one who has made suggestions in this area.

Best wishes as you create resilient families while moving in kindness through brokenness.

From our thriving family to yours,
Deborah and John Lahman

RESOURCES

When we look back at our experiences over the years we know and have admitted in the book that we couldn't have done it alone. We have utilized the expertise of friends and experts. We would be remiss if we didn't share some of those resources we used and some current ones that can help you on your journey to grow and empower your family. This list is not exhaustive however it is a great place to start. Keep asking...keep learning...keep building.

- Active Parenting Publishers by Dr. Michael Popkin at activeparenting.com
- Drive-A-Logue, Family Conversation Game by Adam Brooks
- Children the Challenge by Dr. Rudolph Dreikurs
- Homework Without Tears by Lee Carter and Lee Hausner
- How to Raise an Adult by Julia Lythcott-Haims
- Identity Vs. Role Confusion by Eric Erikson
- Love and Logic Parenting Skills and Techniques at loveandlogic.com

- Owning Up by Rosalind Wiseman
- Seven Habits of Highly Effective People by Steven Covey
- The Self Driven Child by William Stixrud and Ned Johnson
- Unselfie by Dr. Michele Borba

www.ingramcontent.com/pod-product-compliance
Lightning Source LLC
Chambersburg PA
CBHW071218090426
42736CB00014B/2879